First World War
and Army of Occupation
War Diary
France, Belgium and Germany

24 DIVISION
72 Infantry Brigade,
Brigade Machine Gun Company
9 March 1916 - 28 February 1918

WO95/2215/2

The Naval & Military Press Ltd
www.nmarchive.com
Published in association with The National Archives

Published by

The Naval & Military Press Ltd

Unit 10 Ridgewood Industrial Park,

Uckfield, East Sussex,

TN22 5QE England

Tel: +44 (0) 1825 749494

www.naval-military-press.com

www.nmarchive.com

This diary has been reprinted in facsimile from the original. Any imperfections are inevitably reproduced and the quality may fall short of modern type and cartographic standards.

© **Crown Copyright**
Images reproduced by permission of The National Archives, London, England, 2015.

Contents

Document type	Place/Title	Date From	Date To
Heading	WO95/2215/2		
Heading	72nd Machine Gun Coy Mar 1916-Feb 1916		
Heading	Entrained Grantham for overseas 9th March 1916 72 Brigade Machine Gun Company March 1916.		
Miscellaneous	The D.A.G., 3rd Echelon, The Base	06/06/1916	06/06/1916
War Diary	Grantham	09/03/1916	09/03/1916
War Diary	Southampton	10/03/1916	10/03/1916
War Diary	Havre	11/03/1916	12/03/1916
War Diary	Poperinghe	14/03/1916	14/03/1916
War Diary	Ouderdon	14/03/1916	17/03/1916
War Diary	La Levrette	21/03/1916	27/03/1916
War Diary	Dranoutre	28/03/1916	30/03/1916
Heading	72nd Machine Gun Company April 1916		
War Diary	H.Q. Beaver Hall	01/04/1916	01/04/1916
War Diary	N31.a.95.Sheet 28	04/04/1916	30/04/1916
Heading	72nd Machine Gun Company. May 1916		
War Diary	Kammel Wulverghem	01/05/1916	31/05/1916
War Diary	T6b54. T5d94 1/2 T 5d23 T3b 7 1/2 1/2	30/05/1916	30/05/1916
War Diary	South	02/05/1916	02/05/1916
War Diary	No30 C 42 N29 d 51. N34 b 92 N33 b 26	16/05/1916	16/05/1916
Heading	72nd Machine Gun Company. June 1916		
Miscellaneous	D.A.G. 3rd Echelon.	01/07/1916	01/07/1916
War Diary		01/06/1916	29/06/1916
Heading	72nd Machine Gun Company. July 1916		
War Diary	Wulverghem	01/07/1916	01/07/1916
War Diary	Locre	02/07/1916	08/07/1916
War Diary	Petit Pont	11/07/1916	31/07/1916
Heading	72nd Machine Gun Company August 1916		
War Diary	Morlancourt	01/08/1916	01/08/1916
War Diary	Sandpit Area E. 18.d.	10/08/1916	10/08/1916
War Diary	Trenches	14/08/1916	18/08/1916
War Diary	Trenches to Minden Post	19/08/1916	20/08/1916
War Diary	Trenches	21/08/1916	22/08/1916
War Diary	Citadel	25/08/1916	25/08/1916
War Diary	Dernancourt	27/08/1916	27/08/1916
War Diary	Ribemont Sur L'Ancre	30/08/1916	30/08/1916
Heading	72nd Machine Gun Company September 1916		
War Diary	Trenches Delville Wood Dernancourt	05/09/1916	07/09/1916
War Diary	Monfliers	08/09/1916	19/09/1916
War Diary	Hucliers	21/09/1916	25/09/1916
War Diary	Houdain	26/09/1916	26/09/1916
War Diary	Camblain L'Abbe	30/09/1916	30/09/1916
Heading	72nd Machine Gun Company October 1916		
Heading	72nd Machine Gun Company From 1st October 1916 to 31st October 1916 Volume One		
War Diary	Camblain L'Abbe	01/10/1916	01/10/1916
War Diary	Trenches (Berthonval Sector)	04/10/1916	04/10/1916
War Diary	Trenches	11/10/1916	19/10/1916
War Diary	Gouy Servins to Mazingarbe Trenches 24	23/10/1916	24/10/1916
War Diary	Hulluch Sector		

War Diary	Philosophe		
War Diary	Mazingarbe	25/10/1916	25/10/1916
War Diary	Noeux Les Mines	27/10/1916	27/10/1916
War Diary	Trenches	29/10/1916	29/10/1916
War Diary	Hulluch Sector		
Heading	72nd Machine Gun Company November 1916		
Heading	War Diary of 72nd Machine Gun Company From 1.11.16 to 30.11.16 Volume 1		
War Diary	Trenches Hulluch Sector	01/11/1916	28/11/1916
Heading	72nd Machine Gun Company December 1916		
Heading	War Diary of 72nd Machine Gun Company From 1.12.1916 to 31.12.16 Volume 1		
War Diary	Trenches Hulluch Sector	01/12/1916	30/12/1916
Heading	War Diary of 72nd Machine Gun Company From 1.1.17 to 31.1.17		
War Diary	Trenches (Hulluch Sector)	01/01/1917	31/01/1917
Heading	War Diary of 72nd Machine Gun Company From 1.2.17 to 28.2.17 Volume 2		
War Diary	Trenches Hulluch Sector	01/02/1917	03/02/1917
War Diary	Trenches Hulluch Sector and Mazingarbe	12/02/1917	13/02/1917
War Diary	Allouagne (Rest Billets)	13/02/1917	28/02/1917
Heading	War Diary of 72nd Machine Gun Company From 1.3.17 to 31.3.17		
War Diary	Allouagne	02/03/1917	02/03/1917
War Diary	Bully Grenay & Calonne Sector (Map 1. 36c. S.W.1.)	03/03/1917	28/03/1917
Heading	72nd Brigade Machine Gun Company 24th Division April 1917		
Heading	War Diary of 72nd Machine Gun Company From 1.4.17 to 30.4.17		
War Diary	Trenches Double Crassier and Calonne Sector.	01/04/1917	13/04/1917
War Diary	Trenches German Front Line System S.E.of Double Crassier	13/04/1917	15/04/1917
War Diary	Trenches German Front Line System	15/04/1917	15/04/1917
War Diary	City St. Pierre	16/04/1917	19/04/1917
War Diary	Bully Grenay Fosse 10 Petit Sains		
War Diary	Fosse 10	20/04/1917	20/04/1917
War Diary	Allouagne to Ligny Lez Aire	21/04/1917	25/04/1917
War Diary	Glem	26/04/1917	30/04/1917
Heading	War Diary of 72nd Machine Gun Company From 1.5.17 to 31.5.17 Volume 2		
War Diary	Glem. Dennebroeucq 1st Army Special Draining Area	01/05/1917	09/05/1917
War Diary	Ligny Lez Aire Boeseghem	10/05/1917	10/05/1917
War Diary	Boeseghem	12/05/1917	12/05/1917
War Diary	Boeschepe	13/05/1917	13/05/1917
War Diary	Brandhoek & Trenches Hooge Sector	15/05/1917	15/05/1917
War Diary	Trenches Hooge Sector From Trenches 10 Brandhoek	29/05/1917	30/05/1917
Heading	War Diary of 72nd Machine Gun Company From 1.6.17 to 30.6.17 Volume 2		
War Diary	Devonshire Camp (G.22.b.5.9) & Trenches	01/06/1917	05/06/1917
War Diary	Trenches Front of 47 Division	07/06/1917	07/06/1917
War Diary	Devonshire Camp and Trenches	11/06/1917	15/06/1917
War Diary	Micmac Camp (H.31.b.3.5)	16/06/1917	16/06/1917
War Diary	Trenches Mont Sorrel Sector	20/06/1917	21/06/1917
War Diary	Micmac Camp (H.31.b.3.5.) and Trenches	23/06/1917	28/06/1917
War Diary	Trenches and Micmac Camp	28/06/1917	30/06/1917

Heading	War Diary of 72nd Machine Gun Company From 1.7.17 to 31.7.17 Volume 2		
War Diary	Watterdal (Training Area)	01/07/1917	17/07/1917
War Diary	Watterdal to Renescure	17/07/1917	17/07/1917
War Diary	Renescure to Eecke	18/07/1917	18/07/1917
War Diary	Eecke to Nr Steenvoorde	19/07/1917	19/07/1917
War Diary	Steenvoorde to Reningheist Area	20/07/1917	20/07/1917
War Diary	G.32.d.6.7 to Micmac Camp H.31.d and Trenches.	21/07/1917	21/07/1917
War Diary	Trenches (Details in Col. No.4)	22/07/1917	30/07/1917
War Diary	Trenches and Micmac Camp (H.31)	29/07/1917	29/07/1917
War Diary	Trenches	31/07/1917	31/07/1917
Heading	War Diary of 72nd Machine Gun Company From 1.8.17 to 31.8.17 (Volume 2)		
War Diary	Trenches	01/08/1917	04/08/1917
War Diary	Trenches & Micmac Camp H.31.b.5.3.	06/08/1917	07/08/1917
War Diary	Micmac Camp H.31.b.5.3.	08/08/1917	08/08/1917
War Diary	Dickebusch H. 29.d.9.7	11/08/1917	11/08/1917
War Diary	Trenches	15/08/1917	15/08/1917
War Diary	Zillebeke Trench Map 1/10000	16/08/1917	19/08/1917
War Diary	Trenches & Micmac Camp	19/08/1917	20/08/1917
War Diary	Dickebusch H.29.d.9.7.	23/08/1917	23/08/1917
War Diary	Trenches	27/08/1917	31/08/1917
War Diary	Micmac Camp		
Heading	War Diary of 72nd Machine Gun Company From 1.9.17 to 30.9.17 (Vol. 2)		
War Diary	Trenches and Micmac Camp H. 31.b.5.3.	01/09/1917	04/09/1917
War Diary	Dickebusch H.29.d.9.7.to Trenches.	07/09/1917	11/09/1917
War Diary	Micmac Camp H.31.b.S.3. to Strazeele (Merris Area)	13/09/1917	14/09/1917
War Diary	Strazeele	15/09/1917	20/09/1917
War Diary	Caestre to Miraumont Then 13 Beaulencourt Area N.18.a.3.1.	21/09/1917	25/09/1917
War Diary	Haut Allaines Area	26/09/1917	27/09/1917
War Diary	Trenches Villeret Sector	28/09/1917	28/09/1917
War Diary	Villeret Sector	28/09/1917	28/09/1917
Heading	War Diary 72nd Machine Gun Coy. October 1917 Vol 19		
War Diary	Trenches	01/10/1919	31/10/1919
Heading	72nd Machine Gun Company. War Diary October 1917 Appendices		
Operation(al) Order(s)	Operation Order No.2	24/10/1917	24/10/1917
Miscellaneous	Correction to Operation Order No. 2	24/10/1917	24/10/1917
Heading	72nd Machine Gun Company War Diary November 1917 With Appendix.		
War Diary	Trenches	01/11/1917	30/11/1917
Operation(al) Order(s)	72nd Machine Gun Company Operation Order No. 4	18/11/1917	18/11/1917
Heading	72nd Machine Gun Coy for the month of December 1917		
War Diary	In the Field	01/12/1917	31/12/1917
Operation(al) Order(s)	Operation Order No. 5 72nd Machine Gun Company.	20/12/1917	20/12/1917
Heading	72 Machine Gun Coy War Diary for the Month of January 1918		
War Diary	In the Field	01/01/1918	31/01/1918
Operation(al) Order(s)	Operation Order No. 6	01/01/1918	01/01/1918
Miscellaneous	Operation Order No. 7	03/01/1918	03/01/1918
Operation(al) Order(s)	72 Machine Gun Coy Operation Order No. 8	11/01/1918	11/01/1918
Operation(al) Order(s)	Operation Order No. 9	27/01/1918	27/01/1918

Heading	72nd Machine Gun Company War Diary February 1918		
War Diary	In the Field	01/02/1918	28/02/1918
Miscellaneous	for O/C 72nd. Machine Gun Company		
Operation(al) Order(s)	72nd Machine Gun Company Operation Order No. 12	25/02/1918	25/02/1918

words/sus/2

24TH DIVISION
72ND INFY BDE

72ND MACHINE GUN COY.
MAR 1916 - FEB 1918

72nd Brigade 24th Division

Entrained Grantham for overseas 9th March 1916.

72nd BRIGADE

MACHINE GUN COMPANY.

MARCH 1916

Feb 18

To The D.A.G.
    3rd ECHELON.
        BASE.   6:6:16.

Enclosed please find
WAR DIARIES of the 72nd
Machine Gun Company
for MARCH and APRIL,
1916, compiled as
accurately as possible by
me from details supplied
by officers in the Company.
Hoping this is satisfactory.

                    W.K. Pirie
                    Captn.
Comdg. 72nd I.B. Machine
            Gun Company.

72nd Machine Gun Company.

WAR DIARY for NOVEMBER 1916
or
INTELLIGENCE SUMMARY

Army Form C. 2118.

add 15 Vol 1 24
72 M.G. Coy

Place	Date	Hour	Summary of Events and Information	Remarks and references to Appendices
GRANTHAM	9th		Entrained for SOUTHAMPTON. Officers:- Capt T. HUTCHESSON. Lt. F.B. SUTHERLAND. Lt. T.R. REID.	
SOUTHAMPTON	10th		Embark on Transport "BELLEROPHON". 1st Lt F.D. CARGILL. 2nd Lt H.S.C. BARBER. 2nd Lt M.A. TORRIS.	
HAVRE	11th		Disembark & proceed to N°1 Camp. 2/Lt G.H. WHITWORTH. 2/Lt C.D. DIXON. 2/Lt F.E. GILDERTHORPE.	
			2/Lt GILDERTHORPE sick to Hospital.	
HAVRE	12th		Entrained for POPERINGHE.	
POPERINGHE	14th		Detrained & marched to OUDERDOM.	
OUDERDOM	14th – 16th		Parties of all ranks proceed to Salient. (HOOGE & SANCTUARY HOOD SECTOR) for instruction.	
	17th - 27th		Two Guns in action at YEOMANRY POST near ZILLEBEKE. Teams under instruction	
LA LAVRETTE	21st		Remainder of Company move to LA LAVRETTE from OUDERDOM.	
	26th		Took over position for Machine Gun at SHELL FARM. N° 36 C.O.9. (Sheet 28)	
			" " " " SOUVENIR FARM. J5 d57 (do do)	
BRANDHOEK	28th		Move from LA LAVRETTE & take over from 1st CANADIAN BDE Machine Gun Company in line	
			& at BEAVER HALL. Lt F.B. SUTHERLAND in command.	
	30th		Capt. HUTCHESSON sick to BASE.	

W.K. Tillie Capt
Comdg. 72nd Machine Gun Company.

24th Division
72nd Brigade

72nd MACHINE GUN COMPANY

APRIL 1916

72nd Machine Gun Company

WAR DIARY
or
INTELLIGENCE SUMMARY
(Erase heading not required.)

Army Form C. 2118.

April 1916.

Instructions regarding War Diaries and Intelligence Summaries are contained in F.S. Regs., Part II. and the Staff Manual respectively. Title pages will be prepared in manuscript.

Place	Date	Hour	Summary of Events and Information	Remarks and references to Appendices
H:Qrs: BEATER HALL	1		72nd Brigade Machine Gun School of Instruction started.	
	4		2/Lt. GILDERTHORPE returns to duty.	
n31.a.95 Sheet 28.	7/8th night	Positions taken over from CANADIANS	
			SHELL FARM. n36 c18. (Sheet 28) (2nd Gun)	
			FORT PIXIE (2 Guns) T.5.6.6.6 (-.-)	
			BATTLEAXE FARM. n35 c59 (-.-)	
	14th		Capt. HUTCHESSON to duty from BASE.	
	5/30th		Company forms 2nd line of Defence on 72nd Brigade's frontage.	
			Posn. Northern Boundary: N30 C42; N29 d 51; N34 b 92; N33 6.2.6. N32 a 10.8. } Sheet 28.	
			Southern Do, T2 6.54; T5 d 9.4½; T4 d 23; T3 6.7½.	
	30/31st night		Enemy released GAS on a front of 350 yards. N. of MURFERGHEM.	
			Owing to our artillery fire the enemy was only able to make small raids on the Brigade's frontage which raids were easily dealt with and repulsed.	
	12:45 am		2/Lt. GILDERTHORPE slightly wounded & gassed.	
			5 O.R. wounded. 6 O.R. gassed.	

S.H. Sitwell Capt.
72nd Machine Gun Company

O.C. 72nd Machine Gun Company

24th Division
72nd Brigade

72nd MACHINE GUN COMPANY.

M A Y   1 9 1 6.

72nd Machine Gun Company

WAR DIARY
or
INTELLIGENCE SUMMARY.

Army Form C. 2118.

MAY 1916.

XXIV Vol 2
72 M G Coy

Place	Date	Hour	Summary of Events and Information	Remarks and references to Appendices
KEMMEL			During the month the Company has formed the 2nd Line of Defence in the 72nd Infantry Brigade area. 8 Guns being in Strong Points just behind the Trenches & 8 Guns being in Billets all to Reinforce in 50 Minutes.	
LOCRE LOCRE HEAD	1st & 27th		72nd I.B. Operation Orders do not mention the Company as our positions are permanent. G.O.	
	30th April 1st & 15th	12.50 Am	The enemy discharged GAS Smoke his Trenches opposite our front, a raid followed. Enemy easily ejected. We had very few Casualties. 2 men temporarily sick from GAS, no deaths. 2/Lt. E. GILBERTHORPE slightly wounded. G.O.	
			CAPT. W.K. TILLIE. RTD. 7/8NT. 8th R. WEST KENT RGT. Still are Command of Company.	
	2nd		CAPT. T. HUTCHESSON. G.O.	
	16th		2/Lt. L. LAMB. reported for Duty. G.O.	

W.K. Tillie Capt.
Comg. 72nd M. Gun Company.

24th Division
72nd Brigade.

72nd MACHINE GUN COMPANY.

JUNE 1916

To D.A.G.,
    3rd ECHELON.

                                1st July, 1916.

    Herewith WAR DIARY of the 72nd Infantry Brigade Machine Gun Company, for the month of JUNE, 1916.

                                Captain,
                    Comdg. 72nd Machine Gun Company.

Army Form C. 2118.

72 M G Cy Vol 3

WAR DIARY
or
INTELLIGENCE SUMMARY.
(Erase heading not required.)

JUNE 1916.   72ND MACHINE Gun Coy.

Place	Date	Hour	Summary of Events and Information	Remarks and references to Appendices
	1st June		72nd M.G. Company continued to hold the same line as in MAY 1916. 143. 2nd line of Defence to 72nd Infantry Brigade. Exactly same arrangements as in MAY. Continued.	
	10th June	12:40 am	Enemy Shelled G.P.S. from his trenches from about points in their trenches in Squares N.30 & N.36. (BEAUVAL-FRANCE Sheet 20 S.E.). Front line shelled also. Company had no Casualties. Enemy did not fire his trenches. Enemy artillery feeble. ex?	
	17th		2/Lt E. CRUDGETHORPE Sick to hospital. ex?	
	28/29		A party of 8th Battn. The Queens R.R. raided enemy trenches about Point N.36 Central. 5 Prisoners taken. We released 2 Gas Clouds. 2 Guns of the Company (Brns) the LEFT flank of the Raiding party. N.6522a. Cy. S. Major H.F. SMITH in charge of these 2 guns has Slightly wounded, to hospital. ex 9.	
	29th		72nd I.B. Operation order No. 53. 29th June 16. para : 1. "The 72nd Infantry Brigade will be relieved in the trenches on the nights 30th June/1st & 1st/2nd July 16 & 1st/2nd July 1916, by the 7th Australian Brigade & the 174 Infantry Brigade. on Relief the Brigade will move into billets at KORTEPYP & SECRE. as shown on attached title. ex 2.	

Folio 2.

Army Form C. 2118.

WAR DIARY
or
INTELLIGENCE SUMMARY.
(Erase heading not required.)

171st Machine Gun Company.

June 1916.

Place	Date	Hour	Summary of Events and Information	Remarks and references to Appendices
	29th		Ref: 72nd Inf: Brigade Operation Order No. 55 29th June 1916. Para: 7. "The 72nd Inf: Brigade Machine Gun Company will be relieved by part of the 171st Machine Gun Company" by part of 7th & Australian Inf: Brigade Machine Gun Company on 2/7/1916. W.E.D.	

72nd Inf.Bde.
24th Div.

WAR DIARY

72nd MACHINE GUN COMPANY.

J U L Y

1 9 1 6

72nd Machine Gun Company

WAR DIARY or INTELLIGENCE-SUMMARY

Army Form C. 2118.

July 1916.

72 M.G.C. Vol 4

Place	Date	Hour	Summary of Events and Information	Remarks and references to Appendices
WULVERGHEM	1st		The 72nd Machine Gun Company continuing to hold the same line in support of the 72nd Infantry Brigade. Was relieved on night 2/3rd July by	
LOCRE	2/3rd		the 19th Machine Gun Company on the Left Sector & by the 7th Australian Brigade Machine Gun Company on Right Sector of the line held by this Company. The whole Company on Relief moved to Billets in LOCRE area M20.b.2.4.	Sheet 28
	8th		The 72nd Machine Gun Company took over the line of positions held by part of the 2nd & 7th Australian Brigade Machine Gun Companys. The front was hung, trenches C3 & 14, & inclusive, trenches 140 – 136 inclusive. " 135, 134 & Martin Trench. The ½ Company not in the above-mentioned line moved to PETIT-POST FARM (T32.b.22) Sheet 26.	
PETIT POST	17th	10 P	The front held by 72nd Infantry Brigade was readjusted as follows :- Right Boundary :- From front line trench C2055 R. DOUVE to Road Junction U.1.b.2.1. inclusive, MINTER TRENCH, thence along thence to RED LODGE, along main road to PETIT POST and T25 Central.	72nd Inf. Bgde Operation order 57

T2134. Wt. W708—776. 500000. 4/16. Sir J. C. & S.

72nd Machine Gun Company

WAR DIARY
or
INTELLIGENCE SUMMARY.
(Erase heading not required.)

Army Form 2118.

July 1916. (Continued)

Instructions regarding War Diaries and Intelligence Summaries are contained in F.S. Regs., Part II. and the Staff Manual respectively. Title pages will be prepared in manuscript.

Place	Date	Hour	Summary of Events and Information	Remarks and references to Appendices
R.G.H.Q. Point.			Boundary between Right & Centre Brigades the DEULE-EGLISE - MESSINES Road	
			So far as St QUENTIN Cabaret inclusive & thence forward up road L.K.?	
	20.7		The 72nd Machine Gun Company was relieved by the 59th Machine Gun Company night of 20/21st. The 72nd Machine Gun Company on Relief moved to Billets at PIBROUCK (R21 C50) L.K.?	
	24.7		The 72nd Machine Gun Company entrained at BAILLEUL WEST & detrained at LONGEAU at 8 p.m. & marched to Rest Area & Billet at OISSY, arriving morning of 25.7	
	30.7		The Transport & Baggage Wagons moved at 9 p.m. by road for MORLANCOURT (Somme Army)	
	31.7		The Company marched to AILLY-SUR-SOMME entraining for MERICOURT	
			The Company detrained at MERICOURT at 6.30 p.m. and marched to MORLANCOURT staying night there L.K.?	

24th Division
72nd Brigade.

72nd MACHINE GUN COMPANY.

AUGUST 1916

Army Form C.2118.
74 Div
Vol S

WAR DIARY
or
INTELLIGENCE SUMMARY. 72nd Machine Gun Company.
(Erase heading not required.)

AUGUST. 1916.

Instructions regarding War Diaries and Intelligence Summaries are contained in F. S. Regs., Part II. and the Staff Manual respectively. Title pages will be prepared in manuscript.

Place	Date	Hour	Summary of Events and Information	Remarks and references to Appendices
	1916 Aug.			Vide operation orders
MERICOURT	1	6 pm	The 72nd MACHINE GUN COMPANY moved from MERICOURT to the SANDPIT AREA. E.18.d. (Sheet. 62.d.N.E.) to Rest Camp. W.P.	66
SANDPIT AREA E.18.d.	10		The 72nd MACHINE GUN COMPANY moved from the SANDPIT AREA to TRENCHES in front of GUILLEMONT and relieved the 166th MACHINE GUN COMPANY. The 72nd MACHINE GUN COMPANY'S TRANSPORT moved to HAPPY VALLEY L.3.a. (Sheet 62.d.N.E.) W.P.	70
TRENCHES	14		1 N.C.O. to MACHINE GUN SCHOOL. EAULERS, on a VICKERS machine gun course. W.P.	
	16	5.40 pm	Two Guns of 72nd MACHINE GUN COMPANY were placed at the disposal of the C.C. 9th Batn. EAST SURREY REGT. in their attacking TRENCHES S.30.f.72. to S.30.f.7½.4½. SUNKEN ROAD, and TRENCH running parallel and EAST of SUNKEN ROAD. B.M. 2nd Lieut. C.D. DIXON sick to HOSPITAL.	76
"	17		1 SECTION of COMPANY moved from TRENCHES to MINDEN POST (F.18.c.6.4.) W.P.	
	18		On the night 18th/19th the manning 3 SECTIONS of the COMPANY	

CONTINUED.

Army Form C. 2118.

WAR DIARY
or
INTELLIGENCE SUMMARY.
(Erase heading not required.)

72nd Machine Gun Company.

AUGUST 1916.

Instructions regarding War Diaries and Intelligence Summaries are contained in F. S. Regs., Part II. and the Staff Manual respectively. Title pages will be prepared in manuscript.

Place	Date	Hour	Summary of Events and Information	Remarks and references to Appendices
TRENCHES	1916 Augt 18		moved to MINDEN POST. F.18.c.6.4. CASUALTIES. 1 o.r. KILLED. 3 o.r. WOUNDED. 1 GUN KNOCKED OUT.	
MINDEN POST.	19.		2 SECTIONS of 72nd MACHINE GUN COMPANY moved to TRENCHES from MINDEN POST. 2 GUNS relieved 2 GUNS of 73rd MACHINE GUN COMPANY in the QUARRY GUILLEMONT. The remainder of the 72nd MACHINE GUN COMPANY moved from MINDEN POST to LE BRICQUETERIE and CASEMENT TRENCH. 2nd Lieut. J. LAMB WOUNDED.	
"	20			
TRENCHES	21		The Guns of the Company were disposed of as follows for the attack made by the 8th Batn. QUEEN'S ROYAL WEST SURREY REGT. 2 MACHINE GUNS under 2/Lt. LAMB at QUARRY to be at disposal of O.C. 8th QUEEN'S to follow up this attack. 2 MACHINE GUNS under 2/Lt. WHEATLEY to report to O.C. 8th QUEEN'S at QUARRY at 12 NOON. 2 MACHINE GUNS in KNOT TRENCH to move to QUARRY as soon as attack has been launched, with the primary object of meeting any counter attack	vide Operation Order No 79

Army Form C. 2118.

WAR DIARY
INTELLIGENCE SUMMARY

72nd Machine Gun Company

AUGUST 1916.

Place	Date	Hour	Summary of Events and Information	Remarks and references to Appendices
TRENCHES	21		" on the right flank. 2 Machine Guns at about S.24.c.6.4. to provide covering fire over GUILLEMONT — GINCHY and GUILLEMONT — COMBLES ROAD. 2 Machine Guns in GUILLEMONT ALLEY about S.30.a.7.5. in observation, and covering right flank of attack."	made Order No. 79.
	22		Owing to the attack of 8th Queen's not succeeding, the 4 guns under 1/Lt Lant and Wheatley had to withdraw with the infantry when they retired to the original front line TRENCH beside the QUARRY. The 72nd Machine Gun Company were relieved on the night 22/23rd by the 55th Machine Gun Company and moved to the CITADEL.	
CITADEL	25	9.30 a.m.	The Company marched from the CITADEL to DERNANCOURT to bivouacs.	81
DERNANCOURT	27	7.0 p.m.	The Company moved from DERNANCOURT to billets at RIBEMONT sur L'ANCRE.	

Army Form C. 2118.

WAR DIARY
or
INTELLIGENCE SUMMARY.
(Erase heading not required.)

72nd Machine Gun Company

AUGUST, 1916.

Place	Date	Hour	Summary of Events and Information	Remarks and references to Appendices
	1916 Augt			
RIBEMONT Sur L'ANCRE	30	5.30am	The 72nd MACHINE GUN COMPANY moved to RESERVE CAMP at F.S.A. Two sections of Company relieved the 43rd M.G. COMPANY Appnd.Q. N° 84. in the DELVILLE WOOD SECTOR v.f. The remaining half company moved to positions in MONTAUBAN.	

E. Hutt
Lt.
Captain,
Comdg. 72nd Machine Gun Company.

24th Division
72nd Brigade.

72nd MACHINE GUN COMPANY

SEPTEMBER 1 9 1 6

WAR DIARY
or
INTELLIGENCE SUMMARY. 72nd MACHINE GUN COMPANY.

Army Form C. 2118.

24 / Vol 6

SEPTEMBER, 1916.

Place	Date	Hour	Summary of Events and Information	Remarks and references to Appendices
	1916			
	SEPTEMBER			
TRENCHES	5		The 72nd MACHINE GUN COMPANY were relieved in the trenches on the night of 5th and 6th by the 166th MACHINE GUN COMPANY	W.D.O.O. No 87
RENELLE WOOD				
DERNANCOURT	6		The 72nd MACHINE GUN COMPANY moved by road on the afternoon of 6th to DERNANCOURT AREA.	87 M.S.
	7	10.30 a.m	The Company entrained at EDGEHILL and journeyed to KONCORE where they detrained and marched to MONTELIERS. Here they moved into REST BILLETS	M.S.
			The Transport Section of the Company moved from DERNANCOURT for MONTELIERS by road in the 72nd I.B. Transport Column	88 M.S. M.S.
MONTELIERS	8		The Transport of the Company arrived at MONTELIERS in the early evening.	M.S.
	19	8.50 a.m	On the move of the 72nd Infantry Brigade into the 1st ARMY AREA the 72nd MACHINE GUN COMPANY entrained at ABBEVILLE and journeyed to BRYAS where they detrained and marched to HUCLIERS into REST BILLETS.	M.S.

CONTINUED SEPTEMBER, 1916. WAR DIARY or INTELLIGENCE SUMMARY. 72nd MACHINE GUN COMPANY.

Army Form C. 2118.

Place	Date	Hour	Summary of Events and Information	Remarks and references to Appendices
	1916			
	SEPTEMBER			
HUCHERS	21		6532, Sgt REEVES .E. awarded MILITARY MEDAL in JUNE last, and since awarded BAR to same.	WD
			1 ot proceeded on LEWIS GUN COURSE, LE TOUQUET, ETAPLES.	WD
"	22,23	3 p.m.	4 GUNS and TEAMS were moved by motor lorry to BAZORLE SWITCH which place the 4 GUNS and TEAMS garrisoned (Sheet 36 B.S.E. X 16 b and 17a)	WD
"	24	9 a.m.	The 72nd MACHINE GUN COMPANY marched from HUCHERS to HOUDAIN	WD
"	25		1 officer and 1 o.r. proceeded on VICKERS M.G. COURSE, CAMIERS	WD
HOUDAIN	26	7 a.m.	The 72nd MACHINE GUN COMPANY marched from HOUDAIN into Divisional Reserve Area at CAMBLAIN L'ABBE, where they were billeted.	WD
CAMBLAIN L'ABBE	30		6301. Sgt. BASSINGTHWAITE. H.T. awarded MILITARY MEDAL 8836. a/Sgt. ANDERSON, G. ditto 5828. Pte. EAYRE. C.W. ditto	WD WD WD

J Whitworth Lieut. MC
Comdg 72nd Machine Gun Company

24th Division
72nd Brigade

72nd MACHINER GUN COMPANY

OCTOBER 1 9 1 6

24 Vol 7

Confidential

War Diary

of

2nd Machine Gun Company.

From 1st October, 1916. To 31st October 1916.

(VOLUME ONE.)

Army Form C. 2118.

WAR DIARY
or
INTELLIGENCE SUMMARY: 72nd Machine Gun Coy.

OCTOBER 1916

Place	Date	Hour	Summary of Events and Information	Remarks and references to Appendices
CAMBLAIN L'ABBÉ	1916 Oct 1st		Coy proceeded to ABBEVILLE to undergo an Advanced Transport Course.	
TRENCHES 4th (BERTHONVAL SECTOR)	4th		The 72nd M.G. Coy relieved the 17th M.G. Coy in the line, (BERTHONVAL SECTOR). The 17th M.G Coy relieved the 6 guns and teams of the 72nd M.G Coy in BATAILLE SWITCH, X.16a. and 17.b. (Sheet 36 G. S.E.). Three of the relieved guns teams took up positions in the Reserve Line, and the remaining gun teams returned to BILLETS at VILLERS au BOIS. Transport lives at GOUY SERVINS. 14 Guns were in the line in BERTHONVAL SECTOR. 7 of these were in positions situated in the front line and the remaining 7 guns were in support and in the Reserve line.	vide OO 91
Trenches	11th		Intersectional reliefs were carried out by this Company during the 11th.	vide OO 92

Army Form C. 2118.

WAR DIARY
or
INTELLIGENCE SUMMARY.   72nd Machine Gun Coy.
(Erase heading not required.)

OCTOBER 1916

Instructions regarding War Diaries and Intelligence Summaries are contained in F. S. Regs., Part II. and the Staff Manual respectively. Title pages will be prepared in manuscript.

Place	Date	Hour	Summary of Events and Information	Remarks and references to Appendices
	1916		CONTINUED.	
TRENCHES	15th		1 Officer and 2 o.r. proceeded on a Machine Gun Course at CAMIERS.	sx?
"	19	a.m.	On the 72nd Infantry Brigade moving into Divisional Reserve the 72nd M.G.Coy were relieved in the line by the 73rd M.G.Coy. On relief the 72nd M.G.Coy moved into BILLETS at GOUY SERVINS.	sx?
GOUY SERVINS to MAZINGARBE TRENCHES	23	10.30 a.m.	The 72nd M.G.Coy marched to MAZINGARBE and were billeted there the night 23/24.	sx?
	24th	8 a.m.	The 72nd M.G.Coy relieved the 120th M.G.Coy in the line during the day 24th. Eight guns were in the forward trenches and Reserve Line position, and 5 guns were situated in VILLAGE LINE. G. 16.d.-23.a.-23.c.-29.a. (Sheet. 36cNW.3.)	vide OO. 94.
HULLUCH SECTOR				
PHILOSOPHE			3 Guns and teams in BILLETS in reserve at PHILOSOPHE.	
MAZINGARBE	25		The Transport Section of 72nd M.G.Coy moved from MAZINGARBE to NOEUX les MINES.	sx?
NOEUX les MINES	27		From NOEUX les MINES the Transport Section moved to LES BREBIS.	sx?

WAR DIARY
or
INTELLIGENCE SUMMARY

72nd Machine Gun Company

OCTOBER 1916

Place	Date	Hour	Summary of Events and Information	Remarks and references to Appendices
	1916		CONTINUED.	
TRENCHES.	29		Two Guns of 72nd M.G. Coy. in VILLAGE LINE were moved to positions in the RESERVE LINE, thus leaving 3 Guns in the VILLAGE LINE. This move was approved of by the B.G.C. 72nd I.B. Bde?	
HULLUCH SECTOR.				
	1/11/16			

Price
Lt.
Captain
Comdg. 72nd Machine Gun Company.

24th Division
72nd Brigade

72nd MACHINE GUN COMPANY

NOVEMBER 1916

Vol 8

Confidential

War Diary

of

72nd Machine Gun Company.

From 1 : 11 : 16.   To 30 : 11 : 16.

(Volume 1.)

Army Form C. 2118.

WAR DIARY
or
INTELLIGENCE SUMMARY
(Erase heading not required.)

NOVEMBER 1916. 72nd MACHINE GUN COMPANY.

Place	Date	Hour	Summary of Events and Information	Remarks and references to Appendices
TRENCHES. HULLUCH SECTOR.	1916 Nov. 1		The 72nd MACHINE GUN COMPANY continued to support the 72nd INFANTRY BRIGADE in the line in the HULLUCH SECTOR.	
"	2		2/Lieut. H.S.C. BARBER, Transport Officer, sick to Hospital.	
"	8		CASUALTIES :- KILLED 1 o.r. WOUNDED: Lieut. G.A. WHITWORTH and 1 o.r. All by SHELL FIRE.	
"	10		1 o.r. proceeded on MACHINE GUN COURSE at MACHINE GUN SCHOOL, CAMIERS.	
"	18		2/Lieut. H.S.C. BARBER to duty from Hospital.	
"	20		2/Lieut. H.S.C. BARBER sick to Hospital.	
"	22		2/Lieut. C.L. DEWHIRST reported for duty.	
"	23		1 o.r. proceeded on an Advanced TRANSPORT COURSE at ABBEVILLE.	
"	25		Temp. Captain W.K. TILLIE, Comdg. 72nd MACHINE GUN COMPANY, to be Temp. Major while employed with the MACHINE GUN CORPS, to date 1st October, 1916.	

Army Form C. 2118.

WAR DIARY
or
INTELLIGENCE SUMMARY.
(Erase heading not required.)

72nd MACHINE GUN COMPANY.

NOVEMBER 1916.

Place	Date	Hour	Summary of Events and Information	Remarks and references to Appendices
	1916		CONTINUED.	
TRENCHES	25		CONT.D	
HULLUCH SECTOR	27		vide THE LONDON GAZETTE dated 25th November 1916. 2 O.R's proceeded on a MACHINE GUN COURSE at the MACHINE GUN SCHOOL, CAMIERS.	
"	28		2/Lieuts. H.B. HINDLEY and F. MORRIS reported for duty.	

B.T. Lee
Major,
Commanding 72nd Machine Gun Company.

1st December 1916.

24th Division
72nd Brigade

72nd MACHINE GUN COMPANY.

DECEMBER 1 9 1 6.

Vol 9

CONFIDENTIAL

War Diary

of

72nd Machine Gun Company.

From:- 1. 12. 1916.   To:- 31. 12. 1916.

(Volume 1)

Army Form C. 2118.

WAR DIARY
or
~~INTELLIGENCE SUMMARY~~
(Erase heading not required)

72nd MACHINE GUN COMPANY.   DECEMBER. 1916.

Instructions regarding War Diaries and Intelligence Summaries are contained in F. S. Regs., Part II. and the Staff Manual respectively. Title pages will be prepared in manuscript.

Place	Date	Hour	Summary of Events and Information	Remarks and references to Appendices
TRENCHES	1 to 31		The 72nd MACHINE GUN COMPANY continued to support the 72nd INFANTRY BRIGADE in the line	
HULLUCH SECTOR.			in HULLUCH SECTOR.	
			Much indirect fire was carried out during the month on the tramways, tracks and dumps in the enemy's lines.	
"	6		2/Lieut. J.M. KEANS reported for duty.	
"	23		1 or. wounded by SHELL FIRE.	
"	26		1 officer proceeded on a machine gun course at the M.G. SCHOOL, CAMIERS.	
"	30		1 or. wounded by SHELL FIRE.	

31/12/16

W.B. Petrie, Major;
Commanding 72nd Machine Gun Company.

Vol 16

Confidential.

War Diary

of

72nd Machine Gun Company

from 1:1:17   to 31:1:17

(Volume 2)

WAR DIARY
or
INTELLIGENCE SUMMARY.

Army Form C. 2118.

72nd MACHINE GUN COMPANY.

JANUARY 1917

Place	Date	Hour	Summary of Events and Information	Remarks and references to Appendices
TRENCHES (HULLUCH SECTOR)	1917 Jany 1		The 72nd MACHINE GUN COMPANY continued to support the 72nd Infantry Brigade in the HULLUCH SECTOR.	vide ?
	8		Major W.K. TILLIE, Commanding Company, on leave to United Kingdom. Returned 19th January 1917.	vide ?
"	10		2nd Lieut. E. GILBERTHORP sick to hospital.	vide ?
	16		2nd Lieut. J.O. KNIGHT proceeded on course at the 21st Divisional Technical School.	vide ?
	19		2nd Lieut. F. MORRIS sick to hospital.	vide ?
	26		2nd Lieut. H.B. HINDLEY proceeded on course at the First Army A.A. Group.	vide ?
	28		2nd Lieut. F. MORRIS to duty from hospital.	
	31st		Throughout the month much indirect fire was carried out on the roads, tramways, trenches and dumps in the enemy's lines.	vide ?

W.K. Tillie Major,
Comdg. 72nd Machine Gun Company.

1/2/17

Confidential

Vol XI

War Diary

of

72nd Machine Gun Company

From 1.2.17.   To 28.2.17

(Volume 2).

Army Form C. 2118.

WAR DIARY
or
INTELLIGENCE SUMMARY.
(Erase heading not required.)

FEBRUARY 1917   72nd MACHINE GUN COY.

Instructions regarding War Diaries and Intelligence Summaries are contained in F. S. Regs., Part II. and the Staff Manual respectively. Title pages will be prepared in manuscript.

Place	Date	Hour	Summary of Events and Information	Remarks and references to Appendices
	1917			
TRENCHES - HULLUCH SECTOR	1		The 72nd MACHINE GUN COMPANY continued to support the 72nd Infantry Brigade in the HULLUCH SECTOR.	
	3		2nd Lieut. T.O. KNIGHT sick to hospital, whilst on a 4th course of Instruction at the Divisional Technical School.	
"	16	9am	The 72nd MACHINE GUN COMPANY were relieved in the trenches by the 111th Machine Gun Company. On relief the 72nd MACHINE GUN COMPANY moved to MAZINGARBE to Billets for one night.	72 S.B. Op. Order 116
MAZINGARBE				
"	13	9am	The 72nd MACHINE GUN COMPANY marched from MAZINGARBE to ALLOUAGNE (V.26.c and d map.: BETHUINE combined sheet. Edition 6). The Company entered Rest Billets	MARCH TABLE 72 S.B. B.O.116
ALLOUAGNE (Rest Billets)	26		2/Lieut. H.E. DUCKEN and 1 o.r. proceeded to the machine Gun School - CAMIERS - for a machine Gun Course.	
"	13 to 28		While the 72nd MACHINE GUN COMPANY was in rest, a programme of Training was carried out which included:- Tactical Schemes and Exercises, Physical Drill	

T2134. Wt. W708-778. 500000. 4/15. Sir J. C. & S.

Army Form C. 2118.

WAR DIARY
or
INTELLIGENCE SUMMARY.
(Erase heading not required.)

72nd MACHINE GUN COY.

FEBRUARY 1917

Place	Date	Hour	Summary of Events and Information	Remarks and references to Appendices
	1917		Continued.	
ALLOUAGNE	13		Revolver Practice; Firing on Range; Gun Drill &c.	
(Rest Billets)	16		Two courses of Instruction were also arranged.	
	28		(i) Advanced Course for the Senior N.C.O.s of the 72nd M.G. Coy.	
			Company under Lieut. N.A. JOHNS, 72nd M.G. Corps.	
			(ii) Elementary Course for the more backward gunners of the Company under a senior N.C.O.	

M.K. Tinn
Major
Comdg. 72nd Machine Gun Coys.

1/3/17.

Vol 12

Confidential

War Diary

of

72nd Machine Gun Company

From 1. 3. '17.   To 31. 3. '17.

(Volume 2).

Army Form C. 2118.

WAR DIARY
~~INTELLIGENCE SUMMARY~~
(Erase heading not required.)

72nd MACHINE GUN COMPANY.

MARCH 1917.

Instructions regarding War Diaries and Intelligence Summaries are contained in F.S. Regs., Part II. and the Staff Manual respectively. Title pages will be prepared in manuscript.

Place	Date	Hour	Summary of Events and Information	Remarks and references to Appendices
	1917 MARCH			
ALLOUAGNE	2	8-15 a.m.	The 72nd MACHINE GUN COMPANY marched from ALLOUAGNE to BULLY GRENAY, into temporary billets.	72nd I.B's O.O. 118 & attached MARCH TABLE
BULLY GRENAY.	3		The 72nd INFANTRY BRIGADE relieved the 3rd CANADIAN INFANTRY BRIGADE in the line on the CALONNE SECTOR, and were supported by the 4th 72nd MACHINE GUN COMPANY who relieved the 3rd CANADIAN MACHINE GUN COMPANY.	
CALONNE SECTOR (MAP:- 36.c.SW.1.)	4		The 72nd MACHINE GUN COMPANY had 12 guns permanently in action and 4 guns in reserve at BULLY GRENAY. Company Headquarters were at BULLY GRENAY. Transport lines at LES BREBIS.	Do.
"	16		2nd Lieut. J.O. KNIGHT returned to duty off sick leave.	
"	18		The number of guns in the line permanently in action, increased to fourteen; leaving two in reserve at BULLY GRENAY.	
"	19		Lieut. F.B. SUTHERLAND and 2 O.R. proceeded to CAMIERS for a machine gun course.	
"	26		2nd Lieut. H.B. HINDLEY reported sick to F.A.	
"	28		1 officer (2nd Lieut. C. HOPPIE) 2 guns and teams attached to 72nd MACHINE GUN COY.	

T2134. Wt. W708—776. 500000. 4/15. Sir J. C. & S.

Army Form C. 2118.

WAR DIARY
or
INTELLIGENCE SUMMARY.

(Erase heading not required.)

72nd MACHINE GUN COMPANY.

MARCH. 1917.

Place	Date	Hour	Summary of Events and Information	Remarks and references to Appendices
CALONNE SECTOR & BULLY GRENAY. (Map: 36c.SW.1)	1917. MARCH 28.		CONTINUED. Company from 191st MACHINE GUN COMPANY. The 72nd MACHINE GUN COMPANY fired from 4,000 to 5,000 rounds nightly on to enemy's back area, during the month. A system of barrage fire has been installed, whereby fire can be brought to bear on enemy's front line trenches in front of the 72nd Infantry Brigade's SECTOR. J. Ivi Lieut. & Major. Comdg. 72nd Machine Gun Company. 1/4/17.	5.g.

72nd BRIGADE MACHINE GUN COMPANY

24th DIVISION

APRIL 1917

Confidential.

War Diary

of

2nd Machine Gun Company.

From 1st/1917 to 30th/1917.

Volume 2.

Army Form C. 2118.

WAR DIARY
or
INTELLIGENCE SUMMARY.
(Erase heading not required.)

72nd MACHINE GUN COMPANY

APRIL 1917.

Place	Date	Hour	Summary of Events and Information	Remarks and references to Appendices
TRENCHES	1917 APRIL			
DOUBLE CRASSIER 1. and CROWNE SECTION			The 72nd MACHINE GUN COMPANY continued to support the 72nd INFANTRY BRIGADE who were holding the line from the DOUBLE CRASSIER to the BURNING BYNG.	MAP. 36.c.S.W.I.
			The 72nd MACHINE GUN COMPANY had 16 machine guns permanently in the line, including 2 guns and teams attached to 72nd M.G.Coy from 191st M.G.COY. The 2 remaining guns were in reserve at Company Headquarters, BULLY GRENAY. (map Reference:- M.I.C.I.8. (Sheet 36.c.S.W.I.)	36.c.S.W.I. Gav.
"	5		2nd Lieut. W.H. ST.J. SLOANE reported for duty from Base Depot.	61.6.
"	11		2nd Lieut. E.R. EVANS reported for duty from Base Depot.	61.6.
	13		On the afternoon and evening of the 13th instant, patrols from the 2 battalions holding the Brigade Front, viz., 9th EAST SURREY REGT. and 8th ROYAL WEST KENT REGT. were sent out towards the German line and reported the withdrawal of the enemy. Arrangements were immediately made whereby 4 machine guns were attached to the above mentioned battalions and supported them in their advance viz:-	

Army Form C. 2118.

WAR DIARY
or
INTELLIGENCE SUMMARY.
(Erase heading not required.)

72nd MACHINE GUN COMPANY

APRIL 1917.

Place	Date	Hour	Summary of Events and Information	Remarks and references to Appendices
	1917 APRIL		CONTINUED.	
TRENCHES. GERMAN FRONT LINE SYSTEM. S.E. of DOUBLE CRASSIER.	13		2 machine guns under 2/Lieut. A.E. WHEATLEY (8th Queens) attached 72nd M.G.Coy) supported 8th ROYAL WEST KENTS. 2 machine guns under T/Lieut. C.L. NEWHIRST supported 9th EAST SURREYS.	
	14		Company Headquarters were moved from BULLY GRENAY (M.1.c.1.8.) to MAROC. (M.3.c. 35-30) (Sheet 36.c. S.W.1.90.) 44th	
	15, 16, 17, 18		From 15th to 18th inclusive, progress was made through CITÉ ST. PIERRE and by the 17th the approximate line held by the 72nd INFANTRY BRIGADE was from FOSSE 12 de LENS inclusive (M.6.d.75.25) to COWDEN TRENCH inclusive. M.12.C. and d. Patrols were pushed forward in front of these two positions. At the junction of COWDEN TRENCH with the BULLY GRENAY - LENS RAILWAY. (M.12.c.5.1.) The 17th INFANTRY BRIGADE joined the 72nd INFANTRY BRIGADE. Machine guns worked in close co-operation with the Infantry during the whole period, but no good targets were encountered	15th:- Left flank of 72nd I.B's Sector - DOUBLE CRASSIER. Right flank of 72nd I.B's Sector. BULLY GRENAY - LENS RAILWAY. M.12.C.5.1.

WAR DIARY or INTELLIGENCE SUMMARY

APRIL 1917   72nd MACHINE GUN COMPANY

Place	Date	Hour	Summary of Events and Information	Remarks and references to Appendices
TRENCHES GERMAN FRONT LINE SYSTEM	1917 APRIL 15th to 18th		CONTINUED. owing to the close nature of the fighting and the absence of any counter-attacks.	
	15		LIEUT. F.B. SUTHERLAND sick to hospital.	
CITÉ ST. PIERRE	16		2/LIEUT. J. HALL reported for duty from BASE DEPOT.	
"	17		1 o.r. wounded by shrapnel.	
			2/LIEUT. E.A. EVANS sick to hospital.	
"	19	6 am	On the morning of the 19th, between 6 and 9 o'clock the 72nd machine Gun Company were relieved on the line by 138th M.G. Coy.	72—L.B.'s O.O. 136. and were Z/be attached
			On relief the Company moved to BULLY GRENAY, and at 6 p.m. moved to FOSSE 10 .. PETIT SAINS. into billets.	
			Transport Lines :- LES BREBIS.	
			2/LIEUT. H.B. HINDLEY returned to duty from hospital.	
BULLY GRENAY. FOSSE 10 PETIT SAINS			Advanced party of 1 officer and 1 o.r. proceeded to ALLOUAGNE by motor bus to arrange billets for Coy.	72 L.B.'s CHIN. dated 18.17.
FOSSE 10.	20	9	The 72nd MACHINE GUN COMPANY marched to ALLOUAGNE into billets.	72 L.B.'s O.O. 137/16.
			The advance party mentioned above proceeded to LIGNY LEZ AIRE	

Army Form C. 2118.

WAR DIARY
OR
INTELLIGENCE SUMMARY.
(Erase heading not required.)

72nd MACHINE GUN COMPANY

APRIL 1917.

Place	Date	Hour	Summary of Events and Information	Remarks and references to Appendices
	1917 APRIL		CONTINUED.	
ALLOUAGNE to	21	10 a.m.	The 72nd MACHINE GUN COMPANY marched from ALLOUAGNE to billets in LIGNY LEZ AIRE and arrived 2 p.m.	vide ADDENDUM to 72 P.35. C.O. 136.
LIGNY LEZ AIRE	23		Advance party of 1 Officer and 1 OR proceeded to GLEM, near COYECQUE to arrange billets for Coy.	
"	25		The 72nd MACHINE GUN COMPANY marched from LIGNY LEZ AYRE to billets at GLEM, near COYECQUE.	
GLEM.	26/4/30		From 26th to 30th a programme of training was carried out in the 1st Army Special Manoeuvre Area (Squares Q.23.24.29.30.35 and 36. vide THÉROUANNE 36a SPECIAL MANOEUVRE AREA MAP. scale 1:40,000). The training consisted of physical drill, foot drill, and tactical schemes, with pack mules and in conjunction with Infantry Companies.	

30.4.17
W.H. Pim
Comdg. 72nd Machine Gun Company

Vol 14

Confidential

War Diary

of

72nd Machine Gun Company

From 1.5.17.   To 31.5.17.

(Volume 1.)

Army Form C. 2118.

WAR DIARY
or
INTELLIGENCE SUMMARY.
(Erase heading not required.)

72nd MACHINE GUN COMPANY

MAY 1917

Instructions regarding War Diaries and Intelligence Summaries are contained in F. S. Regs., Part II. and the Staff Manual respectively. Title pages will be prepared in manuscript.

Place	Date	Hour	Summary of Events and Information	Remarks and references to Appendices
GLEM- PENNEBROEUCQ 1st Army Special Training Area.	1917 May 1		The 72nd MACHINE GUN COMPANY continued to carry out their training programme in the 1st Army Special Manoeuvre Area. Training consisted of physical exercises, revolver practice, gun drill and tactical schemes, using pack animals, in conjunction with the Infantry bttn.	vide map THEROUANNE 1st Army Special Manoeuvre Area.
"	8		to out to 1st Army Rest Camp bttn	
"	9	9 am	The 72nd MACHINE GUN COMPANY moved from the Training Area to LIGNY LEZ AIRE and were billeted in farms to bttn	
LIGNY LEZ AIRE	10	8 and	The 72nd MACHINE GUN COMPANY marched to BOESEGHEM and were billeted in farms to bttn	
BOESEGHEM	12	6 am	Continuing their march to the line, the 72nd MACHINE GUN COMPANY moved from BOESEGHEM to BOESCHEPE bttn	
BOESCHEPE	13	7.30 am	Section Officers reconnoitred the trenches in the HOOGE SECTOR and during the morning the 72nd MACHINE GUN COMPANY marched from BOESCHEPE to BRANDHOEK and were billeted in camps A & B. bttn	vide sketch BELGIUM and FRANCE. 28.9.27

WAR DIARY
INTELLIGENCE SUMMARY

72ⁿᵈ MACHINE GUN COMPANY

MAY 1917

Place	Date	Hour	Summary of Events and Information	Remarks and references to Appendices
BRANDHOEK &	1917 May 15	8 p.m.	CONTINUED. On the night of the 15/16th., the 72ⁿᵈ MACHINE GUN COMPANY relieved the 70th MACHINE GUN COMPANY in the trenches in the	vide French map ZILLEBEKE 28 N.W.4 & N.E.3 parts of
TRENCHES. HOOGE SECTOR.	16.		HOOGE SECTOR, and supported the 72ⁿᵈ INFANTRY BRIGADE. The Company had 13 guns in the line in the support and reserve trenches, and 3 guns in reserve. Company Headquarters:- YPRES (I.8.c.9.0.) Transport Lines:- BRANDHOEK.	
"	19		The enemy obtained direct hit on gun position at ZILLEBEKE HOUSE (I.22.b.8.25.) The sentry was killed. The gun was not damaged.	
			Major W.K.TILLIE to M.G. School, CAMIERS.	
"	26		1 o.r. buried by direct hit on dugout at DUMP HOLE position. The man was killed (I.24.c.7.3.).	
	27		Lieut. M.E. BULCKEN wounded, shell fire	
	28		Captain. M.B. MACGEORGE took over command of 72ⁿᵈ MACHINE GUN COMPANY, vice Major W.K.TILLIE to England.	

Army Form C. 2118.

WAR DIARY
or
INTELLIGENCE SUMMARY.
(Erase heading not required.)

72nd MACHINE GUN COMPY.

MAY 1917.

Instructions regarding War Diaries and Intelligence Summaries are contained in F. S. Regs., Part II. and the Staff Manual respectively. Title pages will be prepared in manuscript.

Place	Date	Hour	Summary of Events and Information	Remarks and references to Appendices
	1917 MAY.		CONTINUED.	
TRENCHES.	19	MN	The 72nd MACHINE GUN COMPANY were relieved by the 89th MACHINE GUN COMPANY on the night of 29/30th.	Sheet 28 1/40,000
HOOGE SECTOR.	9	3am	On being relieved the 72nd MACHINE GUN COMPANY moved to their Transport Lines at BRANDHOEK.	"
From Trenches to BRANDHOEK.	30	2/pm	The 72nd MACHINE GUN COMPANY marched to DEVONSHIRE CAMP taking over huts from 73rd MACHINE GUN COMPANY. (G.22.b.7.9.) Lieut. F. MORRIS returned from hospital.	

REINFORCEMENTS. ETC.

| | 18 | | Lieut. C.J. YEO and 2/Lieut. J.T. RICHARDS from Base Depot. | |
| | 20 | | Lieut. W. KAY. proceeded on leave to UNITED KINGDOM. | |

W. McGee(?) Captain.

1 June 1917. Commanding 72nd Machine Gun Company.

No 15

Confidential.

War Diary

of

72nd Machine Gun Company.

(From 1. 6. 1917)   (To 30. 6. 1917.)

Volume 7

Army Form C. 2118.

WAR DIARY
or
INTELLIGENCE SUMMARY
(Erase heading not required.)

73rd MACHINE GUN COMPANY

June 1917.

Instructions regarding War Diaries and Intelligence Summaries are contained in F. S. Regs., Part II. and the Staff Manual respectively. Title Pages will be prepared in manuscript.

Place	Date 1917	Hour	Summary of Events and Information	Remarks and references to Appendices
DEVONSHIRE CAMP. (C.22.6.5.9.)	June 1.		The 72nd MACHINE GUN COMPANY were at Devonshire Camp, temporarily attached to the 47th Division.	ZILLEBEKE and WYTSCHAETE TRENCH MAPS. Scale 1/10,000. 28. S.W. 28. N.W. BELGIUM.
" Trenches	2 6 5		The 73rd M.G. Coy relieved the 73rd M.G. Coy in the line, and prepared their positions for barrage fire to support the 47th Division during the impending attack.	
	5.		2 ors wounded. Coy Headquarters were at MELVILLE SUBWAY (I.33.b.). The Transport Lines remained at DEVONSHIRE CAMP.	
TRENCHES FRONT of 47th DIVISION.	7	3 a.m.	On the morning of the 7th June the 47th Division attacked the enemy's trenches during which the 73rd M.G. Coy fired a machine gun barrage on the area attacked by the 47th Division. 2/Lieut. J.O. KNIGHT wounded S.F. Lieut. C.J. YEO wounded S.F. 10 ors wounded.	
DEVONSHIRE CAMP and TRENCHES	11 15		The Transport Lines were moved to NICNAC CAMP. (H.31.6.3.5.) The 73rd M.G. Coy remained in their barrage positions until the morning of the 15th, when 8 guns were withdrawn.	
NICNAC CAMP. (H.31.6.3.5.)	16		The remaining 8 guns were withdrawn from their barrage positions.	

2449 Wt. W14957/M90 750,000 1/16 J.B.C. & A. Forms/C.2118/12.

Army Form C. 2118.

WAR DIARY
or
INTELLIGENCE SUMMARY

(Erase heading not required.)

72nd MACHINE GUN COMPANY. *continued* June 1917.

Place	Date 1917	Hour	Summary of Events and Information	Remarks and references to Appendices
MICMAC CAMP. H.31.c.3.5.	June 16		From the 5th to the 16th June 1917. The total number of rounds fired from barrage positions, while the 72nd M.G. Coy was attached to the 147th Division. was 750,000.	ZILLEBEKE and WYTSCHAETE TRENCH MAPS.
TRENCHES MONT SORREL SECTOR	"		The 72nd M.G. Coy with 7 guns relieved the 70th M.G. Coy on the MONT SORREL SECTOR during the evening of the 10th instant. WM	
	20.		During the early morning of the 20th the 17th M.G. Coy relieved 4 guns of the 72nd M.G. Coy. WM	
	21.		On the night 20/21st the remaining 3 guns were relieved by the 17th M.G. Coy. 1 o.r. wounded.	
MICMAC CAMP (H.31.c.3.5.) and Trenches.	23.		The 72nd M.G. Coy on relief were billeted at MICMAC CAMP. WM The 72nd M.G. Coy relieved the 73rd M.G. Coy in the line on the evening of the 23rd with 13 guns. The remaining 3 guns were held in reserve at MICMAC CAMP. WM	
"	25.		1 o.r. wounded. WM	
"	26.	11pm.	One of our guns in a position in NO MAN'S LAND at KLEIN ZILLEBEKE fired on a German patrol who attacked our bombing post. WM	
"	28		During the night of 28/19th our gun at KLEIN ZILLEBEKE again	

Army Form C. 2118.

WAR DIARY
or
INTELLIGENCE SUMMARY
(Erase heading not required.)

72nd MACHINE GUN COMPANY continued June 1917.

Place	Date	Hour	Summary of Events and Information	Remarks and references to Appendices
Trenches and MICMAC CAMP.	28 & 29.		fired on a German patrol who attacked an advanced post. On the night of 29/30th the 72nd M.G. Coy were relieved by the 69th M.G. Coy. On relief the 72nd M.G. Coy proceeded to MICMAC CAMP.	
"	30	2/pm.	2 Limbers of the 72nd M.G. Coy joined the 71st Infty Brigade Transport and proceeded by road to WATTERDAL. (2nd ARMY REST AREA) The 72nd M.G.Coy and remainder of the Transport entrained at HOPOUTRE SIDING (L.17.d.) (POPERINGHE). and proceeded to the 2nd ARMY REST AREA. The Transport detrained at MIZERNES and proceeded by road to WATTERDAL. The Company detrained at MELLES. and marched to billets at WATTERDAL, arriving about 11 P.m.	

W.M.Gregory
Captain.
Comdg. 72nd Machine Gun Company.

1 July 1917.

Vol 16

WAR DIARY
INTELLIGENCE SUMMARY

Confidential

War Diary

of

71st Machine Gun Company

From 1.7.17. To 31.7.17.

(Volume 7.)

Army Form C. 2118.

WAR DIARY
or
INTELLIGENCE SUMMARY

(Erase heading not required.)

72nd Machine Gun Company.

Place	Date 1917	Hour	Summary of Events and Information	Remarks and references to Appendices
WATTERDAL (Training Area)	July 1 to 17		The 72nd Machine Gun Company carried out a course of training whilst in his Area which included the following subjects. Advanced Gun Drill. Bombing. Firing on Short Range. Revolver Practice. Infantry Drill. Physical Training. Tactical Schemes, with back animals. Lectures. Map Reading. Athletic Practice Attack. WSM	MAP. HAZEBROUCK 5a. and CALAIS 13.
WATTERDAL to RENESCURE	17	2 a.m.	The 72nd M.G. Coy marched from WATTERDAN to RENESCURE Area at about T.9.c.6.1. (Sheet 27). The Coy were billeted in tents. WSM	BELGIUM & FRANCE. SHEET 27. 1/40,000
RENESCURE to EECKE	18	5 a.m.	The Company marched to EECKE (through CAESTRE) and were billeted in barns for the night. WSM	"
EECKE to Nr STEENVOORDE	19	8.30 a.m	The Company moved to near STEENVOORDE and were billeted for the night in barns ... WSM	"

WAR DIARY

~~INTELLIGENCE~~ SUMMARY

JULY. 1917.   72nd Machine Gun Company.

Place	Date	Hour	Summary of Events and Information	Remarks and references to Appendices
STEENVOORDE to RENINGHELST AREA.	20	6.30 a.m.	CONTINUED The 72nd M.G. Coy marched from billets near STEENVOORDE to RENINGHELST AREA and camped in field at G.32.d.6.7. in bivouacs. WMM	BELGIUM & FRANCE SHEETS 27 & 28

G.32.d.6.7 to MICMAC CAMP H.31.d. and TRENCHES.	21.	7.0 a.m.
		
		1.30 p.m.
			The Company moved to MICMAC CAMP. (H.31.d.) and were billeted in tents. WMM
			10 guns & teams proceeded to the trenches as follows and relieved 69th M.G. Coy :-
			  2 guns at KLEIN ZILLEBEKE.
			  1 gun in IMAGE CRESCENT TRENCH.
			  1 gun in IMAGE RESERVE TRENCH.
			  4 guns at I.30.c.30.00.
			  2 guns in IMMOVABLE SUPPORT TRENCH.
			1 o.r. wounded during night of 21st/22nd. WMM
				BELGIUM & FRANCE SHEETS. ZILLEBEKE 1/10000 28.N.W.) 1/
				28.S.W.) 20000

TRENCHES 22 (Details on to Col. No 4.) 30			Details of bombardment remained in MICMAC CAMP. The preparation of BARRAGE POSITIONS was carried out by teams in the trenches. 5 o.r. wounded 25.7.17. WMM	

Army Form C. 2118.

WAR DIARY
INTELLIGENCE SUMMARY
(Erase heading not required.)

72nd Machine Gun Company.

JULY 1917.

Place	Date	Hour	Summary of Events and Information	Remarks and references to Appendices
TRENCHES and MICMAC CAMP. (H. 31.)	29.	4/---	CONTINUED. The remaining 6 guns and teams proceeded to the trenches as follows:- 2 guns under 2/Lt. A.E. WHEATLEY (8th Queen's) relieved the 2 guns at KLEIN ZILLEBEKE. 2 guns under 2/Lt. J. HALL (M.G.C.) relieved the 2 guns at IMAGE CRESCENT and IMAGE RESERVE TRENCHES. 2 guns IMMOVABLE SUPPORT TRENCH. The 4 relieved guns were kept in reserve in LARCH WOOD (W.M.)	TRENCH MAP. ZILLEBEKE 1/10000
TRENCHES.	31.	3.50 A.M.	The 72nd INFANTRY BRIGADE attacked the GERMAN TRENCH SYSTEM with the 1st Batt. NORTH STAFFORDSHIRE REGT. and 8th (S) Battn. THE QUEEN'S R.W.S. REGT. 2 guns attached to 1st N. STAFFS moved as follows:- 1 gun was established 50 yards WEST of GRAVEYARD COTTAGE. 1 gun was placed just EAST of IMAGE CRESCENT. (W.M.) 2 guns attached to 8th QUEEN'S moved to ALARM WEG and took up positions there.	2nd LIEUT. J. HALL. 2nd LIEUT. A.E. WHEATLEY.

Army Form C. 2118.

WAR DIARY
INTELLIGENCE SUMMARY
(Erase heading not required.)

72nd Machine Gun Company.

JULY 1917.

Place	Date 1917	Hour	Summary of Events and Information	Remarks and references to Appendices
TRENCHES	31.		CONTINUED. The 2 guns in ALARM MEG silenced a German machine gun firing from outside a concrete dugout in BULGAR WOOD. During the evening of the 31st, these two guns also assisted in repelling a counter attack on the 41st Division on our right. The 8 guns in barrage positions fired in accordance with Corps Barrage Scheme. Casualties:- 2nd LIEUT. J. HALL. killed by a German sniper. 3 O.R. MISSING. 10 O.R. WOUNDED. 2nd LIEUT. R.E. WHEATLEY. (8th QUEEN'S) slightly wounded, but remained at duty. W/M W.B Margerat Captain. Comdg. 72nd M.G. Company. 5 August 1917.	TRENCH MAP. ZILLEBEKE 1/10000

CONFIDENTIAL

Vol 17

War Diary

of

72nd Machine Gun Company.

From 1.8.17. To 31.8.17.

(Volume 2).

Army Form C. 2118.

WAR DIARY
or
INTELLIGENCE SUMMARY

(Erase heading not required.)

72nd MACHINE GUN COMPANY.   AUGUST 1917.

Place	Date	Hour	Summary of Events and Information	Remarks and references to Appendices
TRENCHES.	1917 1.		The 72nd M.G. Coy continued to support the 72nd Infantry Brigade in the line.	SHEET. 28 BELGIUM & FRANCE.
"	4		10 machine guns of 72nd M.G. Coy were withdrawn & proceeded to MICMAC CAMP. H.31.6.5.3. (sheet 28). 6 guns continued to be manned in the line :-	ZILLEBEKE TRENCH MAP. Scale 1/10000

TRENCHES & MICMAC CAMP. H.31.6.5.3.			1 machine gun in ALARM WEG.
			   1 " " IMPERFECT TRENCH.
			   2 " " KLEIN ZILLEBEKE
			   2 " " HILL 60.	

"	6		At 1.30 a.m. a German prisoner was captured by C/E. PARTRIDGE. S. At 4.0 a.m. A party of Germans raided ALARM WEG and the machine gun in position there had to be withdrawn to KLEIN ZILLEBEKE.	
"	7		On the night of 7th/8th the 72nd M.G. Coy were relieved by the 17th M.G. Coy, who took over the whole BRIGADE	

Army Form C. 2118.

WAR DIARY
or
INTELLIGENCE SUMMARY
(Erase heading not required.)

Instructions regarding War Diaries and Intelligence Summaries are contained in F. S. Regs., Part II. and the Staff Manual respectively. Title Pages will be prepared in manuscript.

AUGUST 1917. CONTINUED.

Place	Date	Hour	Summary of Events and Information	Remarks and references to Appendices
MICMAC CAMP. H.31.6.5.3.	8	—	72ⁿᵈ MACHINE GUN COMPANY. After the relief the 72ⁿᵈ M.G.Coy proceeded to MICMAC CAMP. H.31.6.5.3.	
DICKEBUSCH. H.29.d.9.7	11		The 72ⁿᵈ M.G.Coy moved to DICKEBUSCH into a camp at H.29.d.9.7. and were machine gun company in support.	
TRENCHES	15.	4pm	On the night of 15/16ᵗʰ the 72ⁿᵈ M.G.Coy relieved the 73ʳᵈ M.G.Coy in the line. 8 guns were situated in the front line, 2 in support and 2 in HEDGE STREET TUNNELS. 4 guns were in RESERVE at LARCH WOOD.	
2.H.6.EPRNE TRENCH MAP. 1/10000	16		On the morning of 16ᵗʰ. 6 guns fired in machine gun barrage in conjunction with the attack on the left by the 51ˢᵗ Division. Total no. of rounds fired, 18.000.	
"	18.		A barrage SAA dump of 128.000 rounds was formed in the vicinity of HEDGE STREET.	
"	19		On the night of 19/20 ᵗ the 72ⁿᵈ M.G.Coy were relieved by the	

Army Form C. 2118.

WAR DIARY
or
INTELLIGENCE SUMMARY
(Erase heading not required.)

AUGUST 1917. CONTINUED

Place	Date	Hour	Summary of Events and Information	Remarks and references to Appendices
TRENCHES & MICMAC CAMP.	19 & 20		72ND MACHINE GUN COMPANY:- 73rd M.G. Coy on relief proceeded to Micmac Camp. H.31.c.5.3.	
ANCKEBUSCH H.29.d.9.7.	23		On the evening of 23rd the 72nd M.G. Coy proceeded to Anckebusch at H.29.d.9.7. were machine gun coy. in support.	
TRENCHES.	27		The 72nd M.G. Coy relieved the 73rd M.G. Coy in the line took over the same positions as on the previous tour in the trenches.	
"	30.		Two guns established in Horseboxe's Dugout in support. J.19.c.70.90. (ZILLEBEKE TRENCH MAP).	
MICMAC CAMP.	31		The 72nd M.G. Coy were relieved by the 17th M.G. Coy and proceeded to Micmac Camp. H.31.c.5.3. 20587. Sgt. W.BELL awarded D.C.M.	2/9/17.

W.Macgeorge
Capt. 72nd Machine Gun Coy

Vol 18

Confidential
War Diary
of
72nd Machine Gun Company.

From 1.9.17 to 30.9.17.

(Vol. 2).

Army Form C. 2118.

WAR DIARY
or
INTELLIGENCE SUMMARY.
(Erase heading not required.)

72nd MACHINE GUN COMPANY

SEPTEMBER. 1917.

Instructions regarding War Diaries and Intelligence Summaries are contained in F.S. Regs., Part II. and the Staff Manual respectively. Title pages will be prepared in manuscript.

Place	Date	Hour	Summary of Events and Information	Remarks and references to Appendices
TRENCHES and MICMAC CAMP H.31.6.5.3.	1	-	During the nights of 31 August - 1 September. The 72nd MACHINE GUN COMPANY were relieved in the line by 17th M.G. Coy, and on relief proceeded to MICMAC CAMP. (H.31.6.5.3.)	Sheet 28. and ZILLEBEKE TRENCH MAP. 5M. 1000a.5M.
H.31.6.5.3.	4	6pm	The 72nd M.G. Coy proceeded to DICKEBUSCH CAMP. (H.29.d.9.7.) and sent one m.g. company in Divisional Support	
DICKEBUSCH H.29.d.9.7.	7	night	Moving from DICKEBUSCH on the night of 7/8th the 72nd M.G. Coy	
TRENCHES			proceeded to the line and relieved the 73rd M.G. Coy on the	
MENIN ROAD to SOUTHERN EDGE of BOSMIN COPSE			sector from MENIN ROAD on the NORTH to the SOUTHERN EDGE of BOSMIN COPSE in the SOUTH.	5M. 3M.
BOSMIN COPSE	9	-	2 ORs KILLED. 9 WOUNDED.	
"	11		On the nights of 11/12th the 72nd M.G. Coy were relieved by the 17th M.G. Coy, and on relief proceeded to MICMAC CAMP.	
MICMAC CAMP H.31.6.5.3.			H.31.6.5.3.	5M. 3M.
"	13		2/Lieut. S.M. WILLIAMS reported from BASE DEPOT.	5M.
STRAZEELE	14		The 72 M.G. Coy moved by busses to the MERRIS AREA and were billeted just NORTH of STRAZEELE, on the STRAZEELE - FLETRE ROAD.	5M.
MERRIS AREA				

Army Form C. 2118.

WAR DIARY
or
INTELLIGENCE SUMMARY.
(Erase heading not required.)

72nd MACHINE GUN COMPANY.

SEPTEMBER 1917.

Place	Date	Hour	Summary of Events and Information	Remarks and references to Appendices
STRAZEELE	15		Continued. 2/Lieut. F.J. MILLER reported from Base Depot.	HAZEBROUCK SW J.A. 30
"	18		The G.O.C. of 24th Division inspected the 72nd M.G. Coy.	
"	19		Lieut. N.A. JOHNS proceeded to take over command of 72nd M.G. Coy.	Fell. 10000
"	20	8.30 pm	The 72nd M.C. Coy marched to CAESTRE STATION and entrained.	Fell.
CAESTRE	21	1.10 am	The Company left CAESTRE at 1.10 a.m. and detrained at MIRAUMONT at 10:30 a.m. The Company then marched to BEAULENCOURT AREA (N.18.a.3.1.) and were accommodated in huts.	SHEET 57d Fell. 40000
MIRAUMONT then to BEAULENCOURT AREA N.18.a.3.l.	25	6.20 am	The 72nd M.G. Coy proceeded to the HAUT ALLAINES AREA and were under canvas.	Fell.
HAUT ALLAINES AREA	26	6.30 am	Three Officers of 72 M.G. Coy, proceeded to the line to reconnoitre the VILLERET SECTOR.	Fell.
"	27	8 am	The 72nd M.G. Coy. moved by Buses to BERNES & on the night of 27/28th they relieved the 103rd M.G. Coy in the line in the VILLERET	SHEET 62C HOLNON Fell.
TRENCHES VILLERET SECTOR	28		SECTOR, with R. 5 machine guns in the FRONT LINE, 5 guns	Fell.

Army Form C. 2118.

WAR DIARY
or
INTELLIGENCE SUMMARY.
(Erase heading not required.)

72ⁿᵈ MACHINE GUN COMPANY.

Place	Date	Hour	Summary of Events and Information	Remarks and references to Appendices
			SEPTEMBER 1917.	Sheet 62.c
AMERSET SECTOR.	28	—	Continued — in support and 6 guns in reserve at COTE NOIRS. Coy. Hdqrs:- COTE NOIRS. (L.10.c.30.20) Transport Lines:- MONTIGNY FARM. (K.35.d.95.75)	1/40000

5 Oct 1917.

F. Darby Captain
Comdg. 72 Machine Gun Coy

Vol 19

SECRET

War Diary
72nd Machine Gun Coy.
October 1917

Army Form C. 2118.

Sht/T

WAR DIARY
or
INTELLIGENCE SUMMARY

(Erase heading not required.)

Instructions regarding War Diaries and Intelligence Summaries are contained in F. S. Regs., Part II. and the Staff Manual respectively. Title Pages will be prepared in manuscript.

Place	Date	Hour	Summary of Events and Information	Remarks and references to Appendices
Trenches	1st		72nd Machine Gun Company. a/Capt. R. Gandy took over command of the Coy from a/Capt. Musgrave who is returning to his Battalion. Weather very fine. Enemy quiet.	MSM
"	2nd		Weather still fine. Enemy quiet.	ditto
"	3rd		Lieut. Morris reported from leave and officiated acting 2nd i/c	ditto
"	4th			
"	5th		Our guns co-operated with the artillery in a concentrated shoot on the enemy trenches at noon. Very little retaliation. 2/Lt Dewhurst reported from Base Depot.	MSM
"	6th		Very wet. Enemy quiet.	MSM
"	7th		Little to report. Still very wet	ditto
"	9th		During the night & morning our guns fired 4000 rounds harassing fire on enemy track areas.	ditto
"	10th		Their guns co-operated in an artillery shoot on enemy trenches at 2.30pm no retaliation. Sgt. Jackson accidentally wounded whilst cleaning stores. His Lewis gun stud a round which exploded	MSM

WAR DIARY
or
INTELLIGENCE SUMMARY
(Erase heading not required.)

Army Form C. 2118.

Sheet IV

Place	Date	Hour	Summary of Events and Information	Remarks and references to Appendices
Trenches	18th		72nd Machine Gun Company. Everything very quiet	
"	19th		Lieut. to Stanley Miller 17th M.G.C, reported for duty as second in command of this Coy.	
"	18th		Considerable amount of work done at H.Q. increasing accommodation. Organisation of Coy in a very bad state. State of affairs reported to Bde. H.Q.	
"	15th		2/Lt Harries reported from Base Depot	
"	20th		Court of Enquiry held on staff of Company officers	
"	21st		Enemy artillery activity somewhat above normal	
"	23rd		Received orders re raid to be made by 1st M. Staffs on the night 25/26th. Operation orders issued see Appendix I. Summary of evidence taken on Nr. coy of Nº 8837. Sgt: Sayers H.J.	
"	24th		Very cool by day fine at night. Enemy quiet Preparations for co-operation in raid	
"	25th		Enemy quiet	

WAR DIARY
or
INTELLIGENCE SUMMARY

(Erase heading not required.)

Army Form C. 2118.

Place	Date	Hour	Summary of Events and Information	Remarks and references to Appendices
Trenches	26th		79th Machine Gun Company. 1st N. Staffs carried out raid on enemy trench. In of our guns cooperation giving covering fire. No casualties, 19,600 rds fired. Strength of Coy. 15 O.R. reinforcements reported from Base depot now 11 Officers & 174 O.R.	R.W.M.
"	27th		Enemy attack quiet, our guns fired 1500 rds harrassing fire.	R.S.L.
"	28th		Nothing to report.	R.S.L.
"	29th		Arrangements made with Brigade on our right, re searching Machine Gun fire on No Man's Land when enemy patrols are suspected. During the night our Machine Guns fired 1500 rds harrassing fire on enemy areas.	R.S.L.
"	30th		S.O.R. reinforcements reported from Base Depot. Day wet and cold.	R.S.L.
"	31st		Day very cold. Work continued on Coy H.Q. making stores etc. Nominal strength of the Company on the 31st instant, 11 Officers and 179 O.R's plus 16 O.R's attached for instruction. During Jany Coy. in attempts were successful during the month.	R.S.L. R.D.

2449   Wt. W14957/M90 750,000 1/16 J.B.C. & A. Forms/C.2118/12.

72nd MACHINE GUN COMPANY.

WAR DIARY.

OCTOBER 1917.

APPENDICES.

1. OPERATION ORDERS.

SECRET.   24/10/17

OPERATION ORDER No. 2.

GENERAL SCHEME.

1. A party of the 1st North Staffordshire Regt will raid the
    enemy's trenches between approximately G.14.a.35.88 –
    G.8.c35.20 on night 25th - 26th inst.

CO-OPERATION.

2. The 72nd Machine Gun Company will co-operate with the guns
    and on the targets detailed as follows:-

    No. 1. Gun (L.23.d.70.95) will traverse from
              G.14.a.85.45 to G.14.a.88.03.

    No. 2. Gun (L.23.d.70.95) will traverse from
              G.14.a.65.85 to G.14.a.75.55.

    No. 3 Gun (G.13.b.20.70) will open fire on a bearing
              of 107 degrees Magnetic. Range 700 yards
              This gun will not traverse.

    No. 5 Gun (G.7.b.75.46) will fire on a bearing of
              160 degrees Magnetic. Range 600 yards.
              This gun will not traverse.

    KAFFIR COPSE Guns. These guns will fire on their SOS
              lines with an elevation of 7 degrees. Guns
              will traverse the same amount as for the
              SOS barrage.

FEINT ATTACK.

3. A Feint Attack will be made opposite RUBY WOOD.
    The purpose of this feint is to make as much noise as
    possible in order to divert attention from the operations on
    the right. Two guns of this Company will co-operate
    as follows:-

    No. 6 Gun (G.1.d.68.43) will fire on SOS line
              traversing 10 degrees to the left.

    No 7 Gun (G.1.d.75.75) will fire on SOS line
              traversing 20 degrees to the right.

ZERO HOUR.

4. Zero hour will be the time that the Bangalore Torpedo
    explodes under the enemy's wire. As it is impossible
    to give any definite time for this to happen, all guns
    will wait for the Artillery bombardment to commence before
    opening fire. (The time when the Artillery bombardment
    commences will be the zero hour for the Machine Guns)
    This time will be notified later.

OPERATION ORDER No.2. (contd)

RATE OF FIRE.

5.   For the first five minutes after the opening fire, i.e. Zero - Zero + 5 minutes, the rate of fire for all guns will be 200 rounds per gun per minute.
Z + 5 - Z + 20 = 100 rounds per minute.
Z + 20 - Z + 30 = 200 rounds per minute.

GENERAL.

6.   Flash screens will be used with guns Nos. 1,2,3,5,6 & 7. Belt filling will be carried out by hand.

24th October, 1917.   Commanding 72nd Machine Gun Company.
                                                                    Captain.

SECRET.   24/10/17

Correction to OPERATION ORDER No. 2.

Reference Operation Order No. 2, para 5.

The two guns co-operating in feint on **RUBY** WOOD will fire as follows:-

        ZERO - ZERO + 15 minutes.

        200 rounds per gun per minute.

                                                          Captain

24th October, 1917   Commanding 72nd Machine Gun Company.

W.D. 20

72nd Machine Gun Company.

War Diary.

November 1917

With Appendix.

WAR DIARY or INTELLIGENCE SUMMARY

(Erase heading not required.)

Army Form C. 2118.

Instructions regarding War Diaries and Intelligence Summaries are contained in F. S. Regs., Part II. and the Staff Manual respectively. Title Pages will be prepared in manuscript.

Place	Date	Hour	Summary of Events and Information	Remarks and references to Appendices
Trenches	1st		72 Machine Gun Company. 2/Lieut Hancock & two O.R. proceeded on "Infantry Training Course." Enemy very inactive over M.G's fired 15,000 rds on tracks, roads in back areas	AHA
"	2nd		2/Lieut Dewhurst & 2 O.R. proceeded on leave to U.K. Enemy quiet day wet + cold. M.G's fired 1500 rds during the night.	AHA
	3rd		Dull + wet. M.G's fired 4000 rds.	AHA
	4th			AHA
	5th		2/Lieut Harris rejoined Coy from C.C.S. 2000 rds fired Coy wet + cold. M.G's fired 2500 rds	AHA
	6th		Weather still bad, new emplacements being constructed. M.G.S fired 3500 rds. Lieut Harris & Cpl Dawn proceeded to M.G. School Camiers.	AHA
	7th		Intense fire carried out. 9000 rds fired	AHA
	8th		2/Lieut Herries & 2/Lieut Harris, returned to Base Depot both Officers being supernumerary.	AHA
	9th		Cold wet day. M.G's fired 1500 rds	AHA

WAR DIARY
or
INTELLIGENCE SUMMARY

(Erase heading not required.)

Army Form C. 2118.

Place	Date	Hour	Summary of Events and Information	Remarks and references to Appendices
Trenches	10th		12nd Machine Gun Company. Work done at Coy H.Q. for the lowering of the section entry of the line	ASA
"	11th		Enemy relief completed. 650 rds fired on tracks etc.	ASA
"	12th		Lieut Morris reported from MG School Camiers, recalled as witness on FGCM	ASA
"	13th		Indirect fire as usual. 2000 rds fired	ASA
"	14th		Day cold with thick mist own MG's kept fire on enemy areas all day	ASA
"	15th		8000 rds fired. Lieut Key proceeded on leave & O.R.	ASA
"	16th		Indirect fire as usual. 1000 rds fired. Preparations being made for co-operation in raid to be carried out shortly	ASA
"	17th		Very cold day. AA mounting flucock in Jordan MG's fired 1200 rds	ASA
"	18th		Enemy opened 9000 rds fired by own AA guns at E.A.	ASA
"	19th		Final preparations made for raid, emplacements made & S/A ammo put.. Operation Orders issued (see Appendix No 1).	ASA

Army Form C. 2118.

WAR DIARY
or
INTELLIGENCE SUMMARY

(Erase heading not required.)

Place	Date	Hour	Summary of Events and Information	Remarks and references to Appendices
Trenches	20th		119th Machine Gun Company. Raid carried out by parties of the Battn very successful during which our MGs fired 37,500 rds. Our casualties. 1 O.R. KILLED + 2 O.R. WOUNDED by shellfire. During the day & night of harassing fire, firing 9500 rds	MM
"	21st		Enemy quiet over kept up harassing fire during the day & night firing 10,250 rds. MGs	MM
"	22nd		Day very cold. Co-operated with Artillery in feint attack	MM
"	23rd		Nothing to report. MG carried out usual Indirect Fire 2500 rds fire	MM
"	24th		Situation quiet 5500 rds fired	MM
"	25th		Very windy & cold 2500 rds fired	MM
"	26th		Enemy quiet 2000 rds fired	MM

WAR DIARY or INTELLIGENCE SUMMARY

Army Form C. 2118.

Place	Date	Hour	Summary of Events and Information	Remarks and references to Appendices
Nurlu	28		72nd Machine Gun Company. Day wet & cold, heavy bombardments North Guns MGs fired 2500 rds	NM
"	29		Enemy quiet. Three Officers & 6 N.C.O's of 1st Cavalry Bde reported for reconnaissance and Res Gun MG's fired 3500 rds	NM
"	30		Heavy bombardments on our North flank. All MG's standing to day & night. Our reserve guns (4) at COTE WOOD ordered to TEMPLEUX, and placed under orders of 7.9th M.G.C. Cavalry Machine Gunners ordered back to join their Bdy. Everything on our our front quiet. E.A. flying low & not greatly engaged by our A.A.	NM

SECRET.   18/11/17.

72nd MACHINE GUN COMPANY.

OPERATION ORDER No. 4.

1. Two raids will be carried out on the 72nd Infantry Brigade Front on a date to be notified later. by:-

    (a)   8th The Queens (RWS) Regt. on enemy trenches between G.14.a.3.9. and RAILWAY CUTTING G.8.c.2.3.

    (b)   9th East Surrey Regt. on enemy trenches between G.1.d.90.00 and G.2.c.93.57, for the purpose of inflict- casualties on the enemy. capturing prisoners and obtaining identification.

2. Both raiding parties will enter the enemy trenches at Zero plus 30 secs. Zero hour will be notified later.

3. The 72nd Machine Gun Company will co-operate with the guns and at the targets detailed as follows:-

    (a)   <u>Two guns at SHEPHERDS COPSE.</u>
          Enfilade Fire between QUARRIES from G.14.a.70.40 to G.14.b.00.60.
          Combined sights to be used.
          These guns will not traverse.

    (b)   <u>No. 3 Gun - TURNIP LANE.</u>
          Traverse enemy Front Line (QUARRY TRENCH) from G.14.a.05.55 (Junction of PAN LANE and QUARRY TRENCH) to G.14 a.25.00 (approx).

    (c)   <u>No. 8 Gun - CLUB QUARRY.</u>
          This gun will fire from a position to be selected later.
          Target:- G.2.c.80.85 (Junction of BUCK LANE and SKIN TRENCH)

    (d)   <u>Four Guns - KAFFIR COPSE.</u>
          These guns will fire on SOS lines. Barrage to be lifted on to Eastern Edge of QUARRY WOOD.

    (e)   <u>COLOGNE FARM Gun.</u>
          Traverse BUCKSHOT RAVINE from approximately G.3.c.40.10 (TRENCH JUNCTION) to G.9.a.40.80.

    (f)   <u>No. 6 Gun - BAIT TRENCH.</u>
          Target:- G.2.c.80.85 (Junction of BUCK LANE and SKIN TRENCH)

    (g)   Two guns under 2nd Lieut. Miller will fire from a selected position near GRAND PRIEL WOODS on the following target Combined sights will be used.
          Enfilade G.14.a.30.35. — G.14.a.70.40

4. <u>Opening of Fire.</u>
    All guns will open fire at ZERO.

5. **Programme of Firing.**

   All guns except KAFFIR COPSE.

   Z to Z + 2 min .... 1 Belt.
   Z + 2 to Z + 25 .... 1 Belt per 3 min.
   Z + 25 to Z + 40 min .... 1 Belt per 2 min.

   KAFFIR COPSE GUNS.

   Zero to   )
   Z + 8 mins   ) 1 Belt per 2 Mins.

   Z + 8 to   )
   Z + 25   ) 1 Belt per 4 Mins.

   Z + 25 to   )
   Z + 35   ) 1 Belt per 2 Mins.

   Z + 35 to   )
   Z + 50   ) 1 Belt per 4 Mins.

   Z + 70 to   )
   Z + 76   ) 1 Belt per 2 Mins.

   Z + 90 to   )
   Z + 110   ) 1 Belt per 4 Mins.

   Z + 110 to   )
   Z + 120   ) 1 Belt per 2 Mins.

6. Section Officers will indent on Coy H.Q. for all requirements such as Oil, Four by Two, S.A.A., New Barrels, etc

7. A report on the firing will be sent to Coy H.Q. as soon as possible after completion of programme.

8. Acknowledge.

9. All watches will be synchronised at Coy H.Q. at 8 p.m.

18th November, 1917.

T. Darby
Captain
Commanding 72nd Machine Gun Comany.

Copies to :-
O.C. 72nd M.G.Coy.
2nd in Command, 72nd M.G.Coy.
D.M.G.O.
O.C. No.1 Section
O.C. No. 3 Section.
O.C. No. 4 Section.
War Diary (2 copies)

Vol 21

WAR DIARY

72nd Machine Gun Coy

for the month of

DECEMBER 1917

WITH APPENDICES

WAR DIARY
INTELLIGENCE SUMMARY
(Erase heading not required.)

Army Form C. 2118.

Place	Date	Hour	Summary of Events and Information	Remarks and references to Appendices
In the field	1st		Road Bucquoi-Gun-Tortelary. Captain R. Bagby and two O.R.'s proceeded to No. 16. U.W. Found fresh positions chosen in case of enemy break through. Our front line strong. Improvements on both flanks. Enemy attitude on our front, quiet.	JM
	2nd		Day dry but very cold. Enemy attitude quiet. 2500 rounds fired (indirect). Cavalry M.G. came into 3 Platoon Positions.	JM
	3rd		Very hard frost, difficulty experienced in keeping guns in action, oil freezing hard. 1250 rounds fired.	JM
	4th		Reconnoitred trench areas with B.G.C. Selected time for machine guns 2000 rounds. Lieut W. May returned from leave to U.K.	JM
	5th		Positions chosen for Vickers. Hard frost, enemy shifted out von Aylmer.	JM
	6th		Day cold, freezing hard, R J Morris reported from leave Carnino 3000 rounds fired (indirect)	JM
	7th		Day cold, thawing, enemy attitude quiet, nothing to report	JM
	8th		Day wet and cold, enemy quiet 1500 rounds fired	JM
	9th		Day clean and dry, E.A. active. Artillery active. Withdrew our front line 1000 rounds fired at 6.16. 1500 rounds fired (indirect)	JM

WAR DIARY or INTELLIGENCE SUMMARY

Army Form C. 2118.

Place	Date	Hour	Summary of Events and Information	Remarks and references to Appendices
T.H. Field	10th		2nd Machine Gun Company. Day wet and cold. 1200 rounds fired.	
	11th		Enemy seemed nervy and shelled frequently. 1200 rounds fired.	FM
	12th		Day dry and frosty, enemy shelled heavily all day (attention to trench mor.)	FM
	13th		Day dry but cold. Heavy bombardment on our left.	FM
	14th		Day cold. Our guns fired 1200 rounds (indirect).	FM
	15th		Day cold. Our guns fired 1200 rounds (indirect). Patrols returned from Beaumont Hamel. A new recent position occupied in their ground. Trench E.A. dropped bomb behind Coy Hqrs.	FM
	16th		No Cavalry H.Q.'s reported and reconnoitred the long leg Coy shelled.	FM
	17th		Heavy snow, all quiet.	FM
	17th		All quiet, hard frost and misty. Capt. R. Davy reported from Coy to U.S. Lieut. W.S. Mullet proceeded on tour to U.S.	FM
			All quiet	FM
	19th		All quiet. Evening VIII and advance party reported to Coy Hqrs.	FM
	20th		Company relieved by 5th Cavalry Squadron R.G. Relief completed at 4.30 p.m. Company proceeded to Braquis by motor lorries from Templeux. Strength 20 + 4 + 21 about. Left of the enemy	MW
	21st		Approached our Trench Lamb horden and concealed themselves in a down trench about 15 yds from our own gun. Movement was reported to the commander of the gun team (Sgt Robertson)	MW

WAR DIARY
or
INTELLIGENCE SUMMARY

Army Form C. 2118.

Place	Date	Hour	Summary of Events and Information	Remarks and references to Appendices
E. McJulle 21st			2nd Northumberland Company	AM
			and he went and interviewed the N.C.O. of 7/Lt Infantry Coy/Sects Group. They had nothing to report. He returned to his gun position not satisfied with the situation. He therefore decided to go out in front and see if any hostile parties were concealed anywhere. He ordered a volunteer from his gun team and only one volunteered. 1501S Sgt Robertson J and 10200 Pte Black R went out in front of Thornh Lane and about 10 yards went known on the light with the hostile party. Sgt Robertson & Pte Black were both wounded. Sgt Robertson thought that his bomb exploded in the block when the hostile party was concealed, but nothing was found of a party going out.	
22nd			Cleaning of guns, fixing of tubs etc, for company.	PM
23rd			very hard frost, Church Parade 10 am	PM
24th			Physical Training, Squad Drill, Musketry drill, very hard frost and heavy snow	PM
25th			Xmas Day, Very hard frost, little unusual intervals	PM
26th			Physical Training. Route march Cleaning of Guns, very hard frost.	PM
27th			do do do do do very hard frost, break in weather to 1759.	PM
28th			do do do do do Squad Drill.	PM

WAR DIARY
or
INTELLIGENCE SUMMARY.
(Erase heading not required.)

Army Form C. 2118.

Place	Date	Hour	Summary of Events and Information	Remarks and references to Appendices
St Michell	29th		2nd Machine Gun Company.	
			Inspection by G.O.C. at 10.30 am. Xmas Dinner at 2 pm. Concert by the men at 6 pm.	PM
		11 a.m.	Reinforcements arrived.	
	30th		Day dull. Had first Church Parade at 10 am.	PM
	31st		Digging trench and strong points for flank defence of Maurgies. 2nd Lt. R.B. Hancock returned from leave to U.K. Guard front.	PM

OPERATION ORDER No. 5.
72nd. MACHINE GUN COMPANY.

1. Three Squadrons of the 5th. Cavalry Division will relieve the 72nd. Machine Gun Company on the 21st. inst.,

2. The following guides will be at COTE WOOD at 12 noon on the 21st. inst.,

    KAFFIR COPSE........2 Guides.
    ALL OTHER GUNS......1 Guide per team.

3. All Trench Stores, Maps, Secret Papers, Indirect Fire Tables, S.O.S. calculations etc., will be handed over and receipts obtained. A copy of this receipt will be sent to Company Headquarters.

4. The Nos. 1 of each gun team will remain behind with the relieving team for 24 hours. No. 1 Section will leave behind Cpl. Thorogood and only two Nos. 1. On the expiration of this time all Nos. 1 will report to Cpl. Thorogood at KAFFIR COPSE who will proceed to VRAIGNES via the TRANSPORT LINES. The Transport Officer will provide this party with a guide.

5. All gun boots not yet returned to Brigade Gun Boot Store will be handed over and a separate receipt obtained for same.

6. On completion of relief the Company will move by motor lorry to VRAIGNES.

7. **TRANSPORT.**

    Limbers will report as follows on the 21st. inst.

    8.30am...........2 Limbers.
    10.9am...........4 Limbers.
    2.0pm............Mess Cart.
    3.9pm............3 Limbers.

    These Limbers will all proceed to Company Headquarters, COTE WOOD via TEMPLEUX, and will then proceed to Company Hqrs. VRAIGNES and report to 2nd. Lt. Williams.
    The C.Q.M.S. will pack the meat and other rations to provide the dinner for the Company at VRAIGNES in some of the limbers arriving at 8.30am.

8. Acknowledge.

Issued to:-
1. 2nd. in Command.
2. O.C. No. 1 Section.
3. O.C. No. 2 Section.
4. O.C. No. 3 Section.
5. O.C. No. 4 Section.
6. T.O.
7. C.S.M.
8. C.Q.M.S.
9. War Diary.
10.

K. Darby
CAPTAIN.
Commanding 72nd. Machine Gun Company.

Vol 22

72nd Machine Gun Coy

War Diary

for the month

JANUARY 1918

With Appendices

Army Form C. 2118.

WAR DIARY
or
INTELLIGENCE SUMMARY

(Erase heading not required.)

Place	Date	Hour	Summary of Events and Information	Remarks and references to Appendices
Britteld	1st		Digging trench and strong points for flank defence of Vaulgnes bois touching Rue (St Place) 2nd Lt W Pidgeon return from Course at VII Corps School.	JMcW
	2nd		Company left Vaulgnes to go in support, relieving the 17th Brigade. No 3 & 4 Sections relieved 2 guns in front of Templeux No. 1 & 2 Sections relieved 2 guns at Hervilly.	JMcW
	3rd		Cleaning of guns and equipment small box respirators & P.H Helmet inspection and foot inspection. Capt R Danby reconnoitred trenches. Very cold and hard frost, very slight thaw about mid day	JMcW
	4th		No 1.2.3 Sections under 2nd Lt Dewhirst Mulford & Mothered left Hervilly for the line at 8.30am to relieve daylight positions. Night relief teams left at 2.30pm with Lay. 4pm Relief complete 7.30pm. Very Quiet. Hard frost.	JMcW
	5th		Fairly quiet. Templeux and Guanns shelled at intervals. Lt Mulford shots from leave to U.K. Capt R Danby left for Course at Camiers at 2.30pm Lt W.S Miller took over command of Section in absence. Lt F Morris appointed acting 2nd in Command	JMcW
	6th		Had first situation – Enemy shelled Guanns with 5.9'', 4.2's also a few near Church in Templeux. Enemy planes bombed Peiziel	JMcW
	7th		Threw shelling at entrails of Guanns & Templeux. Gas shelling around Templeux, neighbourhood at 10.0pm and 3.0am. Rain during night.	JMcW

WAR DIARY or INTELLIGENCE SUMMARY

Army Form C. 2118

(Erase heading not required.)

Instructions regarding War Diaries and Intelligence Summaries are contained in F.S. Regs., Part II and the Staff Manual respectively. Title Pages will be prepared in manuscript.

Place	Date	Hour	Summary of Events and Information	Remarks and references to Appendices
In the Field	8th		72nd Machine Gun Company. Enemy 5.9" Howitzer using active in neighbourhood of Quarries and Headquarters. Between 10.10 and 10.25 pm about 70 5.9's fell around by Hqs and the men had to take shelter in the sap. One direct hit was obtained on French Indian Battery's billet (no one injured). Accommodation so so- No. was very bad. 2000 rounds fired. Heavy snow.	JM
	9th		Enemy fired 4.2 Howitzers and Headquarters (at about 3 hours for each 5 minute) a lot shells fell near Templeux Church. Heavy rain during night and very little shelling. 2000 rounds fired on roads and trucks.	JM
	10th		Very hazy weather. Heavy shelling in the vicinity of Templeux during morning. Heavy retaliation by our Artillery. 2000 rounds fired by our M.G's during night.	JM
	11th		Slight thaw during morning, rain during night. Situation normal. 2000 rounds fired by M.G's on trucks and roads.	JM
	12th		Little rain during morning.	JM
	13th		All 17th M.G Coy to recombant. Fairly quiet during the day. Snow during day. Coy relieved by the 17th M.G Coy. Nos 1 & 2 Sections proceeded to Templeux Positions. Remainder of the Coy proceeded to Hervilly.	JM
	14th		Dry day. 2 G.m. sent to Monigny for A.A. duties.	JM

WAR DIARY
or
INTELLIGENCE SUMMARY

(Erase heading not required.)

Army Form C. 2118.

Place	Date	Hour	Summary of Events and Information	Remarks and references to Appendices
In the Field			72nd Machine Gun Company	
	15"		Little rain during night. Working party of 20 men to Mgr Country bohr.	SM
	16"		Wet day. Working party found as 9-15" instant	SM
	17"		Fair day. Working party found as 9-15" instant	SM
	18"		Rain at intervals. Working party found for R.E. Tank Patrol	SM
	19"		Heavy rain. 2nd Lt Muller, A.O.C. and the hos't went to Mabacourt for Alarm Practice	SM
	20"		Fairly day day. Two trips at Tincourt Wood & 2nd Lt Williams in to reginald to reginalin with the Rifle Brigade's nos'd. 2nd Lt Hancock relieved 2nd Lt Williams in the line. hos 1 and 2 Sections at Woreilly by 4 o'pm. Wet day.	SM
	21"		Wet during early morning. 2nd Lt Williams proceeded on leave to U.K.	SM
	22nd		Dull day, all quiet	SM
	23rd		Showery day, very dull	SM
	24"		Fine day. 2nd Lt Muller relieved 2nd Lt Hancock to Tincourt bombing position	SM
	25"		Very quiet day. All quiet	SM
	26"		Fine day. Nothing unusual happened	SM
	27"		Fine day. Enemy planes bombed Montigny Farm vicinity at 11.0 pm with heavy bombs	SM
	28"		Coy. relieved 73rd M.G. Coy in the Line. Relief passed very quiet. Complete by 7.5 pm.	SM
	29"			

WAR DIARY
or
INTELLIGENCE SUMMARY
(Erase heading not required.)

Army Form C. 2118.

Instructions regarding War Diaries and Intelligence Summaries are contained in F. S. Regs., Part II. and the Staff Manual respectively. Title Pages will be prepared in manuscript.

Place	Date	Hour	Summary of Events and Information	Remarks and references to Appendices
Gatchild	30th		72nd Machine Gun Company. During day fairly quiet. 50 rounds fired at Enemy Planes. Very misty while front. Situation quiet.	JM JM
	31st		Reinforcements to Company during month. Strength of Company at end of month Proceeded or been to U.K. during month	O/R 08 — 15 10 — 175 2 — 18	JM JM JM JM

SECRET.   1.1.18.

OPERATION ORDER No. 6.

1. The 72nd. Machine Gun Company will move on the 2nd. inst., to HERVILLY and relieve the 17th. Machine Gun Company.

2. (a) No. 3 Section will relieve the guns at A.B.C and D POSTS
   (b) No. 4 Section will relieve the Section in Reserve at TEMPLEUX.
   (c) 2nd. Lt. R. D. Hancock will be in charge of the above two Sections and will be accommodated by the 73rd. Machine Gun Coy.
   (d) The above Sections will move at 10.0am. on the 2nd. inst., 200 yards interval will be maintained between Sections.
   (e) Guides will be at TEMPLEUX (West End) at 12.45pm.

3. The remainder of the Company will move off at 10.15am. Two hundred yards interval will be maintained between Sections and between each pair of limbers.

4. 2nd. J. G. Hopwood will report with two N.C.O's at HERVILLY at 9.0am.
   2nd. Lt. S. M. Williams will arrange to hand over billets etc., to the Officer of the 17th. Company on arrival.
   The A.A. mounting will be handed over, also all work in progress in trenches.

5. TRANSPORT.
   The undermentioned limbers will report at time shown:-
    8.0am..................3 A and 4 A.
    8.30am.................1 A and 2 A.
    9.0am..................7 Limbers.
    9.30am.................Mess Cart.

6. The Q.M. Stores will move to Montigny independently at 10.30am.

7. RATIONS.
   Rations for Nos. 3 and 4 Sections will be at 73rd. Machine Gun Company Headquarters, TEMPLEUX at 6.30pm. on the night of the 2nd. inst.
   Rations for remainder of Company for the 3rd. inst., will be sent to HARVILLY.

8. 2nd. Lt. R. D. Hancock will report completion of relief to Company Headquarters at HERVILLY.

                  CAPTAIN.
       Commanding 72nd. Machine Gun Company.

Copies to:-

1.	2nd. in Command.	7.	C.S.M.
2.	O/C No. 1 Section.	8.	C.Q.M.S.
3.	O/C No. 2 Section.	9.	Transport Officer.
4.	O/C No. 3 Section.	10.	War Diary
5.	O/C No. 4 Section.	11m	War Diary.
6.	2nd. Lt. Williams.		

SECRET.   3/1/18.
OPERATION ORDER NO 7.
----

1.   The 72nd. Machine Gun Company will relieve the 73rd.
Machine Gun Company on the 4th. inst. in the Front Line Positions.

2.   The 73rd. Machine Gun Company will relieve the 72nd.
Machine Gun Company on the 4th. inst. in the Support Positions.

3.   Half of the Front Line Guns will be relieved in the day-
time and half by night-time.

4.   DAY-TIME RELIEF.

  (a) One gun team of No. 1 Section under 2nd. Lt. Hopwood will
relieve No. 13 Gun (Hargicourt Trench).
  (b) Two guns of No. 2 Section under 2nd. Lt. Miller will
relieve Nos. 14 and 15 Guns (Hargicourt Trench).
  (c) Two gun teams of No. 3 Section under 2nd. Lt. Dewhirst will
relieve Nos. 1 and 6 guns.
  (d) Three gun teams of No. 4 Section will relieve Nos. 4, 5
and 12 teams.
  (e) Guides will be at Company Headquarters TEMPLEUX for Nos.
1, 2 and 3 Sections at 10.0am. and at the Cemetery TEMPLEUX
for No. 4 Section at the same time.
  (f) Limbers will report as follows:-
       7.30am......HERVILLY....2A, 2B, 1A.
       9.0am.......The Cemetery, TEMPLEUX 3A, 4A, 4B.
  (g) The Hervilly party will move off at 8.15am. prompt.

5.   NIGHT-TIME RELIEF INCLUDING HEADQUARTERS RELIEF.

  (a) Three gun teams of No. 1 Section under 2nd. Lt. Rodgers
will relieve Nos. 9, 10 and 11 guns.
  (b) Two guns of No. 3 Section under 2nd. Lt. Williams will
relieve Nos. 2 and 3 Guns. 2nd. Lt. Williams will be at Company
Headquarters, TEMPLEUX at 3.0pm. to take charge of these gun
teams and pack the limber.
  (c) One gun team of No. 2 Section will relieve No. 16 Gun.
  (d) Guides for Nos. 1, 2 and 3 Sections will be at Company
Headquarters TEMPLEUX at 4.0pm.
  (e) Limbers will report as follows:-
       1.30pm - HERVILLY - 1B, 3B, 1C, 2C, 3C, 4C, Headquarters
                           and Mess Cart.
       3.0pm - TEMPLEUX - 2A.
Note:-
       2A Limber will in this case be furnished with a fresh
pair of mules.
  (f) The Hervilly Party will move off at 2.15pm. prompt.

6.   No. 7 Gun Position is not at present occupied. The fourth
gun team of No. 2 Section will therefore remain at Coy. Hqs.

7.   RATION DUMPS.

  (a) 1st. Limber
       No. 1 Section.........Villeret Crucifix at 5.0 pm.
       No. 2 Section(2teams). Forked Roads at L.5.d.15.65.
       No. 3 Section   ) at 5;30pm.
  (b) 2nd. Limber.
       No. 4 Section - Orchard Post at F.22.b.05.40 at 5.0pm.
  (c) 3rd. Limber.
       Company Headquarters and) Company Headquarters, TEMPLEUX
       one team of N. 2 Section) at 5.0pm.

8.   The Nos. 1 of all gun positions are remaining for 24 hours
2nd. Lt. Hancock will arrange for the Nos. 1 of No. 3 Section
to remain at A, B, C and D Posts for the same time

OPERATION ORDER NO 7 (Contd).

9. All Trench Stores, Maps, Work in Progress, S.O.S. Lines and calculations will be taken over.

10. Completion of relief will be reported to Company Headquarters.

R. Darby

CAPTAIN.
Commanding 72nd. Machine Gun Company.

Copies to:-

1. O/C No. 1 Section.
2. O/C No. 2 Section.
3. O/C No. 3 Section.
4. O/C No. 4 Section.
5. Transport Officer.
6. 2nd. in Command.
7. C.S.M.
8. C.Q.M.S.
9. War Diary.
10. " "
11. 2nd. Lt. Williams.
12. 2nd. Lt. Hopwood.

SECRET

72nd Machine Gun Coy.
Operation Order No. 5

The 72nd Machine Gun Company will be relieved in the line by the 17th Machine Gun Company on the 12th inst.

Three guides from Nos. 9, 10, 11 & 16 positions will be at Crucifix L.3.c.80.70 at 11 a.m. On relief these teams will report to Coy HQ. Two other guides from 17th M.G. Coy will meet them and guide them to positions A.B.C. & D.

Limbers for No. 1 Section will be at Crucifix at L.3.c.80.70 at 12.30 p.m.

Four guides from Nos. 4, 5, 6 & 12 positions will be at ORCHARD POST at 1.30 p.m. and guide the 17th Machine Gun Coy's teams to these positions. On relief these teams will proceed to HEKNULY. The limbers for No. 2 Section will be at ORCHARD POST at 3.30 p.m.

Two guides from Nos. 14 & 15 positions will be at the Crucifix L.3.c.80.70 at 3 p.m. On relief these teams will report to Coy HQ and then proceed to Cemetery dug out. One limber for No. 2 Section to be at Crucifix L.3.c.80.70 at 3 p.m.

One guide for No. 13 position to be on road at No. 15 position at 4.45 p.m. On relief this team will report to Coy HQ and proceed to Cemetery dug out. One limber for No. 2 Sec will be on road outside No. 15 position at 5.30 p.m.

4 guides from Nos. 1, 2, 3 & 8 positions will be at ration dump X roads at L.5.d.20.60 at 5 p.m. On relief these teams will proceed to Hennouy. Limbers of No. 3 Section will be at ration dump at 5 p.m.

2 limbers and the Coys transport to report to Coy HQ at 5.30 p.m.

All maps taken over will be left in dug outs together with land lines to be carried.

11.1.18

SECRET.   27/1/18.

OPERATION ORDER No. 2.

The 72nd. Machine Gun Company will relieve the 73rd. Machine Gun Company in the Line on the 29th. inst.

1.   **No. 4 Section** will relieve Positions 9, 10, 11 and 12. Guides from the 73rd. Machine Gun Company will be at CRUCIFIX L.4.d.3.3 at 10.0am.

2.   **No. 3 Section** Guides from A, B, C and D Posts will meet teams of the 73rd. Machine Gun Company at CRUCIFIX L.3.c.7.7 at 12 noon. On being relieved the teams from C and D Posts will proceed to Orchard Post at 3.0pm. and meet guides from the 73rd. Machine Gun Company who will take them to Positions 4 and 5. Guides from the 73rd. Machine Gun Company will be at A and B Dugout at 3.0pm. and take them to 6 and 12 Positions.

3.   **No. 1 Section** Guides from Nos. 14 and 15 Positions will be at CRUCIFIX L.4.d.3.3 at 11.0am. One Limber to be at Company Headquarters at 9.15am.
            Guides from Nos. 7 and 13 Positions at CRUCIFIX L.4.d.3.3. at 5.30pm. One limber to be at Company Headquarters at 3.45pm.

4.   **No. 2 Section** Guides from 1, 2, 3 and 8 Positions at Fork Road L.5.a.2.8 at 5.30p m. Limbers to be at Coy. Hqs. at 3.45 pm.

All Trench Stores to be carefully checked before taking over.
All A.P. S.A.A. to be carefully checked.

                                    W Stanley Miller
                                                              Lieut.
                                    1/c 72nd. Machine Gun Company.

72nd Machine Gun Company

War Diary.

February 1918.

WAR DIARY
or
INTELLIGENCE SUMMARY
(Erase heading not required.)

Army Form C. 2118.

Place	Date	Hour	Summary of Events and Information	Remarks and references to Appendices
12 Machine Gun Coy	1.2.18		Very misty in early morning. Very quiet	MK
	2.2.18		Fine day. Fairly quiet. 1500 rounds fired	MK
	3.2.18		Fine day. Situation normal. 2nd Lt May relieved 2nd Lt J.J. Mullen the latter saw rounds fired on M.G. lines. 2nd Lt J.J. Mullen proceeded on leave.	MK
	4.2.18		Fine day. M/G at night 800 rounds fired on V.G. lines.	MK
	5.2.18		Dull day. 200 rounds fired at T.A.	MK
	6.2.18		Dull day. Coy. temporarily relieved on the line by 17th A.J. bty. and proceeded to Ouagies. Capt R. Booty returned from G.H.Q. Pratt Some Wheat bumper.	MK
	7.2.18		Dull wet day. Nothing to report. Coy. employed in the general cleaning up of kit etc.	MK
	8.2.18		Dull day. Company cleaning guns and gun kit.	MK
	9.2.18		Training commenced.	MK
	10.2.18		Various Company's and H.Q. Section 8.45 am. Physical Drill, Gun Drill, Rifle Drill. 2nd Lt W. Mollet in afternoon.	MK
	11.2.18		Weather change able. Parade as previous day.	MK
	12.2.18		Parade as previous day. Rain during morning.	MK
	13.2.18		Packing of transport etc. accessories etc. left to Doqly's Z.H & M. talked to Manoly to D.A.G.O. of 4th Dismounted Cavalry Brigade to arrange relief.	MK
	14.2.18		Two 1 & 2 Sections relieved Machine Gun & Caution Dug out Group. Very quiet relief.	MK
	15.2.18		Dull day. Quiet. 2nd Lt W. Mullet relinquished O.C. battalion and visited all our positions in afternoon.	MK
	16.2.18			

WAR DIARY
or
INTELLIGENCE SUMMARY

(Erase heading not required.)

Army Form C. 2118.

Instructions regarding War Diaries and Intelligence Summaries are contained in F. S. Regs., Part II. and the Staff Manual respectively. Title Pages will be prepared in manuscript.

Place	Date	Hour	Summary of Events and Information	Remarks and references to Appendices
	7.2.17		2nd Machine Gun Company.	
			Both A Guns returned from an R.T.C. course of four days.	
	25.2.17		Weather fair generally. Enemy quiet. Situation normal. Considerable bombing of back areas by enemy planes.	
	26th		This battalion relieved 11th to 2nd in the 4 Coy in Modena. Relief complete bt 1 pm. Company first to the night at Montigny. Strength of battalion to Montigny on the form area by road & buses. Strength of the 27th inst.	
	27th		Company proceeded to Pontauxcourt by train.	
	28th		Entrainment about 1.30 pm. and marched six miles in the rain to billets. Cleaning up of billets, and preparations for training etc. Billets very good.	

R Karz: Lieut
Off 92nd Machine Gun Company

SECRET   25.2.18

72nd Machine Gun Company
OPERATION ORDER N° 12

1.   The 202nd Machine Gun Company will relieve the 72nd Machine Gun Company on the 26th inst.

2.   All Trench Stores, Maps, S.O.S. and Harassing Fire calculations, detail of Water Supply, rations etc. will be handed over. Ten belt boxes per gun will also be handed over to relieving Company. All belt boxes surplus to this number will be brought out by Sections. Receipts will be obtained for all stores handed over.

3.   GUIDES   Two guides per group of guns will be at Cross Roads at L.15.d.70.98. at 6 p.m. on the 26th inst.

4.   Time of completion of relief will be reported to Coy. H.Q. as early as possible.

     On completion of relief Sections will proceed independantly to MONTIGNY, where the Company will be billeted for the night 26/27th. Guns, Tripods etc. will be carried in the limbers of 204th M.G. Company.

                                          T. Darby
                                               Captain
                          Comdg. 72nd Machine Gun Company.

Copies to:-
1. O.C. N° 1 Section
2. " " 2 "
3. " " 3 "
4) War Diary
5)

www.ingramcontent.com/pod-product-compliance
Lightning Source LLC
Chambersburg PA
CBHW081434160426
43193CB00013B/2281